My Father's Feathers

A Journey of Transformation and Healing, One Feather At a Time

MacKenzie Nelson
#1 International Best Selling Author

My Father's Feathers
A Journey of Transformation and Healing
One Feather at a Time

Copyright © 2022 by MacKenzie Nelson

RHG Media Productions
25495 Southwick Drive #103
Hayward, CA 94544

All rights reserved. No part of this publication may be reproduced distributed or transmitted in any form or by any means including photocopying recording or other electronic or mechanical means without proper written permission of author or publisher, except in the case of brief quotations embodied in critical reviews and certain other noncommercial uses permitted by copyright law.

ISBN 979-8-9867833-0-7 (paperback)
ISBN 979-8-9867833-1-4 (hardcover)

Visit us on line at www.YourPurposeDrivenPractice.com
Printed in the United States of America.

WHAT PEOPLE ARE SAYING

"MacKenzie Nelson is a gifted writer who grabs your attention from the first page. You will laugh, you will cry, and you will fall in love with My Father's Feathers."
—Maureen Ryan Blake, Maureen Ryan Blake Media Productions, Founder of Power of the Tribe

"Never have I been more captivated, encouraged, and felt seen, by a book. MacKenzie's vulnerability and honesty had me hanging on every word."
—Jackie Fahey, Stylist, Daughter, Sister, Wife, Mother, Friend, and Woman

"The author reveals a gutsy vulnerability while sharing a uniquely personal story that will resonate with everyone. You will find peace, healing and joy as the story unfolds."
—Jami Webster Hall, Doctor of Jurisprudence, Modern Mom, Justice Seeker, and Book Club Aficionado

"This story is one that confirms 'love wins' so long as you're willing to go out and fight for it."
—Julia Harriet, MiT Builder of Homes and Dreams, Best-Selling Author

"MacKenzie shares her experiences and unwavering spiritual faith with such a clear, honest vulnerability that is truly inspiring. This book is an amazing resource for anyone looking to jumpstart their own healing and spiritual journey."
—Jennifer Logan PhD, LCPC, NCC, Therapist, LifeStance Health

"MacKenzie Nelson has proven an old adage to be true once again- when you change the way you look at things, the things you look at change."
—Yvonne Greer/Owner, Power Zone Personal Training

"From the very beginning of her life, MacKenzie has had one challenge after another thrown at her and she has overcome every one of them with grace and style!"
—**Mary Horst, Contracting Executive and Friend**

"This is a book that encourages the reader to seek out their own truths and self-knowledge so we can be ready to serve our individual true purpose even better!"
—**Raechelle, Licensed Massage Therapist**

"What an incredibly powerful book! I highly recommend this book if you're looking to heal, be inspired, and to really connect to what it is to live as love."
—**Kara Goss, Author/Speaker/Mentor**

"This book is a journey through pain, persistence and perseverance. Her story is one of reflection with the hopes it can inspire others to not give up."
—**Maureen Famiano President, MEFMedia Author, Best Business Minds of Tampa Bay**

"MacKenzie's book is written simply but holds a powerful, deep message. Her pursuit of wholeness demonstrates a life of overcoming difficulties and achieving peace and impact."
—**Elda Robinson, Best-Selling author of** A Simple Cup of Ty

CONTENTS

Preface 7

Chapter 1: Introduction: Born of Fire 9

Chapter 2: Family Dynamics 13

Chapter 3: Church, Family, and Basketball 17

Chapter 4: Born to Stand Out 23

Chapter 5: God, *The Matrix*, and Destiny 29

Chapter 6: Cuddles 37

Chapter 7: My Choice 45

Chapter 8: Healing, Love, and School 53

Chapter 9: Lincoln and My Grandfather 61

Chapter 10: My Brother's Wedding 67

Chapter 11: Sins of the Father 75

Chapter 12: Medical Challenges and Nevada 81

Chapter 13: Tell Mom, "She is Going to be Okay." 89

Chapter 14: Chronic Pain 95

Chapter 15: Italy 99

Chapter 16: Pain and Freedom 105

Chapter 17: One Day at a Time 111

Chapter 18: Gold Crosses 117

Chapter 19: The Encounter 123

Chapter 20: True Peace 127

Chapter 21: Releasing the Excess 133

Chapter 22: Chloe's House 137

Chapter 23: The Other Side 143
Chapter 24: Life Without Mother 147
Chapter 25: Three Pages A Day 155
Chapter 26: Rewind and Reflect 161
Chapter 27: New Life 165

Closing Thoughts 171
Acknowledgments.. 173
Pinion Points To Help You Grow Your Wings 175
About The Author... 185
Reviews... 187

PREFACE

Thank you so much for purchasing a copy of my book! I felt called to start writing following a spiritual encounter, and this book is the story of my journey. As a matter of fact, when I first started writing three pages a day a few years ago, I didn't know my own story and didn't even realize my capabilities as a writer. Honestly, I've always been a "watch the movie" kind of girl, so I wasn't really even into reading books until I started writing my own. As I continued to stay persistent, I witnessed as my story emerged on the pages and was surprised to find the healing that was unleashed in my own life as a result of putting my thoughts on paper.

This book changed my perspective and continues to change my life in new ways I am constantly discovering. It is my hope that it will do the same for you as you read through my life story and the insights I have gained.

Perhaps one of the biggest discoveries I have made is learning how the same areas of my life where I once felt my wings had been clipped were the very same ones that were now empowering me to soar. As I leaned into what I felt God speaking, He taught me how to live my life from a new, higher perspective – and continues to help me build my wings. I hope this book helps you embrace your story and grow your wings to soar.

To support you, I included a special section in the appendix with special Pinion Points to help you grow your wings. It can be found in the back of the book and is meant to be used as a supplement to the chapters as you read through my story for your own reflection and self-growth. I hope you will utilize these insights, comments, and questions to get the most out of this book as you explore my lived experiences. Please note, I have changed some of the names to protect identities, but the story and my journey are my true experiences – which I hope will serve, encourage, and empower you on your journey.

I have prayed over all the material covered within these pages. Please know that if you can personally relate to some of my experiences, you are not alone. I know firsthand how hard some situations are to walk through without support and feeling like nobody else can understand. I hope you feel encouraged through these pages to know there is a new day dawning, there is hope on the horizon, and healing is possible. Psalms 91:4 "He will cover you with His feathers, and under His wings you will find refuge; His faithfulness will be your shield and your rampart." (NIV Translation)

With Love,
MacKenzie

CHAPTER 1

Introduction: Born of Fire

I'm named after Mackenzie Phillips, an actress from the sitcom *One Day at A Time*. While my mom was pregnant with me, she was watching the rolling credits at the end of the show and loved the name. She told me the main reason she decided not to abort me was because one night, she had a very vivid dream prophesying my birth. She saw me, as a little toddler, running into her arms, and she knew she had just met the little girl in her womb. She always conveyed this matter-of-factly, like an unimpressive, bland detail, when she spoke of it to me. However, to me, as I grew up, it meant I had a purpose. In Gaelic, one of the meanings of my name is "born of fire." I discovered that definitely fit my birth, life, and journey.

What my mother saw that night, which she called a prophesy, I believe was actually a memory: one she hadn't experienced yet in her time, but one that she would have with me, her daughter in the future, after I was born, knew how to walk, and was big enough to run into her arms. The Lord used the gift He had given me while I was in my mother's womb to communicate with my mother to save my life before I was born. I've inherited this gift of dreams and visions.

I could speak full sentences by the age of one, and as soon as I learned how to write, I was in love. I would write and write in those early days. I had so many thoughts, so many questions, and I'd dream up storyline after storyline. I have always been a dreamer, and someone who has always questioned the status quo – the overall process by which society operates.

I was born to stand out, quite literally. I stand at a commanding 6'1" tall, and I've always looked older than my age, especially as a child. Even at the tender age of five, adults would question my integrity when I told them my true age. "You have got to be at least seven or eight," they'd argue back with me, insisting I was fibbing. They'd stare and gawk at my body, looking me up and down. Due to my size, I felt a constant pressure to act older than I actually was. I observed how other "normal-sized" girls were treated, and quickly caught on that my body was different. I was different.

At the age of six, I sat down with my mother and father at our small, wooden kitchen table in our home. I remember feeling like I was in trouble because it was rare to have both of my parents' undivided attention, so I knew whatever they wanted to discuss was a big deal. My heart was in my throat and my palms were sweating while I racked my brain wondering what I had done to require this meeting with both of them. I was bracing myself for the worst when I sat down in that chair, feeling like my wobbly legs might suddenly give out.

The words my mom spoke next would completely shatter me, my identity, and the world as I knew it.

"You have a different father," she stated. She went on to attempt to further explain. "The dad you know and call Paul is not your 'real' father. However, he is the 'real' father of your sister and brother, but not yours."

The words hit the six-year-old me like a ton of bricks and buried me beneath their heavy impact. My head was swimming. I did not possess the necessary coping skills as a young child to process the full depth and meaning of this information. I didn't know what to think and was very scared and confused. What I heard was "This is not your dad. You thought he was, but he isn't. He is still the dad of your siblings, but not yours."

She confirmed what my body had been speaking to me all along: YOU ARE DIFFERENT.

My world crumbled in an instant, though I felt a sense of relief coming off of my mother, as the burden shifted from hers to mine. I have often wondered: Did she tell me this information as a six-year-old for my benefit or for hers? My Dad, Paul, although not biologically my father, signed my birth certificate. He has been my dad since the day I was born.

I stopped writing. I stopped dreaming. I stopped … being a child. I now had adult concerns and worries to contend with and try to sort. At the age of six, my childhood was over.

I also learned my mother had an affair with my uncle. The ugly truth of their affair had surfaced and was no longer a secret. As a result, she worried that my cousin, his daughter, would tell me about the true origins of my biology, as retribution. It was common knowledge when my parents got married that she was already pregnant with another man's baby. It made me greatly resent my father's side of the family. THEY made me feel like this. I also harbored animosity toward my dad, Paul, since my mother pointed to his family as the root cause for devastating my childhood with this biological bombshell.

My relationship with my mother was forever changed from that day forward. She did not get me counseling following the revelation of my true parentage. Instead, she launched a full-throttle campaign in our household to ensure my silence. I became a walking target for her to vent her frustration, her anger at God, her unhappy union with my father, a bad day, anything. I became the scapegoat for her dissatisfaction.

At various points throughout my childhood, I'd try to ask my mother for information about my biological father, to obtain anything about where he was or where I could find him. She would say "He was a very bad man, and you do not want to find him. **He was in the mafia, and if you ever do try and find him, he will kill me for sure and possibly you too.**"

I thought I must have done something very wrong and very bad to be so different from my sister and brother, and for my own biological father to abandon me. Instead of offering a shoulder for me to cry on, or sympathy for the predicament she had dropped into my lap, my mother heavily discouraged me from talking about the subject of my biological father by using scare tactics. Each time I'd ask questions, she'd get noticeably bothered and gave very short answers. Her tone and demeanor would cue me in that this was not something she wanted to talk about, and she would actively shame me for bringing the topic to her attention.

I was confused by her inability to talk about the very information she relayed to me herself. Why did she tell me this and then refuse to talk about it with me? I decided I would not stop asking the questions penetrating my soul and kept pursuing her for answers. I was determined to find out who this man was because I needed to figure out my own identity.

Each time I'd think about my biological father, a surge of emotions would race through me at lightning speed. Anger, resentment, and confusion overwhelmed my soul, like a sea of shattered glass.

When I'd try to sort it out, the pain would well up in me again, releasing the flood of tears I tried so hard to keep contained inside. Who is he? Why isn't he here? What did I do so wrong that he didn't want me? I would cry silent, heaving sobs into my pillow – and when I'd pushed the pain down for too long, scream these questions into the dark.

These sessions, although torturous and leading to no real answers, seemed to be the only thing that would release some of the pressure.

I would go ask my mother for more information, and she would silence me by shaming me further. Her tone would frighten me as she reminded me about how much I was not wanted: "He offered me a brand-new red convertible if I agreed to abort you. He didn't want you. If it weren't for me, you wouldn't be here."

There was never a family or group conversation in our home about the revelation of my paternity. There still hasn't been one, to this very day. As a result, I became the shameful, family secret – and my voice, my ability to process this revelation, were sacrificed. Exchanged for silence.

To this day, I'm not certain how or when my siblings were informed of the fact that I had a different biological father. But when the relentless bullying from my sister started, I knew that she knew. We continue to struggle with our strained relationship to this day.

CHAPTER 2

Family Dynamics

My sister, Ivy, is a year-and-a-half younger than me. She would call me fat or say demeaning things to me regarding my paternity. My mother would often overhear her, and we'd both be told to "play nice" or to "get along." The more my mother backed up my sister's treatment of me, and confirmed that it was okay to mistreat me, the worse my sister acted.

The only time she was corrected for her poor treatment of me was by our dad, Paul. My brother, Owen, is three years younger than me, the baby of the family. My brother and sister shared a much closer bond growing up, I believe because they simply saw themselves as the same, sharing the same biological father.

Suppressed and unprocessed emotions about my biological father tainted everything I did. When the burden was too heavy to bear alone and the pain got too intense, I'd once again risk being on the receiving end of my mother's wrath.

"Where is he? What happened?"

I'd boldly confront my mother, and depending on her mood, I got a variety of responses. Sometimes I was handled roughly or screamed at for simply inquiring. Mostly, though, she'd put me in my room and reply in a lecturing tone: "You have a father, and his name is Paul." Case closed. She would tell me I was a "bad girl" for the tantrums I threw and point me out to my brother and sister as an example not to follow, from a very young age. She established as early on as I can remember that she was infallible, did not make mistakes, and did not tell lies; therefore, if there was an issue, I was the one to blame, and I would suffer the consequences.

Paul worked very long hours on a factory assembly line and picked up additional overtime shifts as frequently as they were offered. He has always been a very hard worker, and was a very traditional husband in every sense. He left the parenting, cooking, and cleaning to my mother, and he brought home the bacon, so to speak.

I earnestly looked forward to him coming in the door. I tried to tell him, as best as I could as a small child, about the treatment I received, but lacked the mature communication skills required to do so. Still, I was desperate for him to hear me, so as soon as he came in the door, I would run as fast as I could and throw my arms around him and refuse to let go. He would tell me to stop, but I wouldn't listen because I was desperate to feel loved.

My mother, while observing my cries for help, would callously comment to my father, "See what I have to put up with all day while you're at work?"

She manipulated situations with my father by reinforcing that I was strong-willed and needed to be broken. She exploited her role as my caretaker by instructing my father to act according to this narrative.

When I was around seven years old, I had become close friends with a neighborhood girl the same age as me. Her parents worked and never seemed to be around much, so we spent a lot of time at her home together unsupervised. She taught me a new game to play with her, but it confused me and hurt me.

Following a slumber party one night at her house, the other girl who was in attendance returned home acting very differently than she normally did, and her parents noticed. They talked to my parents, who in turn questioned me. I answered my parents honestly, thinking nothing had happened, and they didn't suspect any foul play and never brought up the topic again.

What I didn't realize at the time was that due to the sometimes physical, but constantly emotional abuse I was enduring at home, I had normalized pain. When the sexual abuse started, I did not know what it was or how to begin to talk about it.

I struggled to keep a lid on my emotions as a small child because my mother had adopted a culture of silence in our home. I tried so hard to express myself. When I look back, I am now so proud of the little girl that I had been. I see now how hard I fought for my mother to value me and my feelings. I tried over and over and over, relentlessly. If my mother deemed my behavior out of line, she sent me to my room, and her rule was that I could not emerge until I was silent. I screamed in my room until I lost my voice, thinking "SHE WILL HEAR ME ONE WAY OR ANOTHER."

I protested her silent culture for years, craving authentic conversation. I screamed and screamed, alone in my room, barely taking a breath and only leaving when I could sneak out without my mother noticing because I couldn't take the hunger pains, or the fire in my throat burned too badly and I needed water.

When I stopped screaming, my mother would meet me on the outside with a condemning look on her face and a sarcastic, "You done now? What is your problem?"

She wouldn't listen to me speak, so she would hear me scream. She'd hear me fight for my voice and advocate for myself. She could put me in my room, but she could never silence me.

I remember thinking at times that if I keep this up long enough, this might be the time when she'll come in and ask, "MacKenzie, sweetie, what is wrong? Why do you do this?"

Instead, she told me I was too much. Too angry. Too over-emotional. Too sensitive. Her labels were her truth. She needed them to justify her harsh treatment and enforce silence. She ignored my desperate pleas for her love and affection and refused to come inside my room to comfort me.

A lifetime of my mother sweeping instances, emotions, and life in general under the rug had infected me, and now I was under that rug with everything else being suffocated and drowned out by her inability to emotionally function. She did not know how to have conversations where she was willing to learn about me. She had tunnel vision and saw what she wanted to see, and was dead set on asserting her dominance over me. I did everything I could think of to get her attention, but each time I managed an audience with my mother, it was just for more punishment. I couldn't win. I saw at some point I was fighting a losing battle, and everything was stacked against me.

We spent summers at the local pool and went on family vacations to Florida. From the outside looking in, we were the perfect family. My mother always dressed us well, she was beautiful, my dad was handsome, and we were each very attractive children in our own rights. Sometimes, when we were at the pool and she was around her other friends, I would overhear her speaking about me. "I don't know what is wrong with her. She's not a normal child." She'd proceed to humiliate me further by bringing up specific instances. I'd watch with great shame as they would all stop looking at my mother and shift their gazes to me.

In those moments, I desperately wanted to disappear. Now that I am an adult, one of these women my mother regularly had these conversations with remarked to me that she was "surprised I turned out normal."

CHAPTER 3

Church, Family, and Basketball

I was raised in a very religious home. We were Pentecostal and attended an Assemblies of God church twice on Sundays (morning and evening) and every Wednesday night. I loved Jesus very much, even if He didn't necessarily love me like He loved other little girls. Other little girls knew their biological fathers, and my mother made it clear that mine wanted me dead.

I began to draw my own conclusions about the character of the Lord and who He must be based on my own circumstances, and how my mother represented Jesus in our home. "Do as I say, not as I do" was practically her life motto, and she claimed to know Jesus better than everyone. No matter how hard I tried, I could not please my mother and she wouldn't stop hurting me, so I thought God must be the same. I was never going to please God, but I still greatly wanted His love. Not having it hurt.

While in church, I felt obligation and a pressure to perform and be on my very best behavior. My parents made me stand every Sunday morning to sing unending, slow-paced hymns with language like "thou art" for what seemed to be an eternity (at least an hour straight) even though my tiny, aching legs screamed at me to sit down. Events would occur each service that would terrify me. I remember there were flags representing the different countries of the world situated in the front of the church, and women would come and grab the flags out of the blue and randomly run around the auditorium screaming in complete chaos. I never knew when someone was going to fall out of their chair and start violently shaking on the ground and sometimes, someone would yell things in a strange language for no reason at all.

MY FATHER'S FEATHERS

I started throwing huge tantrums nearly every Sunday morning before we left, to avoid having to go to church. But this just got me further punishments. I was forced against my will to attend for years.

I still shudder remembering one Sunday in particular, when my mother violently pulled me from Sunday school. The prior week, I had gotten a blue calligraphy pen that I was absolutely obsessed with. I took that pen with me everywhere, even in the car as we made a family trek out to visit my mother's parents at their farm. I was playfully poking my siblings with it, and she grabbed it out of my hand without warning and tossed it out the window, never to be seen again.

I was devastated, and felt the punishment most certainly didn't fit the crime.

I was reminded of the new leather jacket my mother had purchased, only days earlier. She raved about how much she loved it and was so excited to wear it.

When no one was looking, I seized my chance and went to the hallway closet. It was only fair that I ruin something she loved, since she took what I loved. The silky-butter finish of the jacket glided between my tiny fingertips. I raised the scissors with my right hand, gripped down on them as hard as I could and cut upwards through one sleeve, just a few inches. I didn't go all the way up the sleeve because I only wanted her to feel what I felt, and to understand what she had cost me when she threw out my pen. In my little mind, this seemed like the best way to communicate what she had cost me.

As we were getting ready to leave for church, I watched as she grabbed her now damaged coat out of the closet and quickly put it on. The sense of impending doom gripped me as I was off to Sunday school. Suddenly, my mother showed up, ripped me out of my chair, yanked me roughly down the stairs and through the parking lot, and finally shoved me into the back seat of our car. We flew home at such a high speed I thought we may wreck and die. Terror raced through my heart and dread filled my soul as I tried to figure out what she would do to me next. She opened my door and pulled me out roughly.

She forcibly pushed me into the house and threw me down to the ground and started to kick and punch me. I writhed in pain as the crushing blows impacted my tiny body and screamed for someone to help, but she only hit me harder in response. I crumpled into a ball on the floor and did my best to guard myself from her repetitive blows. She screamed, "You are such a bad child! You are the worst little girl in the whole world! You are a hateful little thing! Why would you think you could do this to my coat? What is wrong with you?" When the beating was over, she tossed me into my room like a ragdoll and left me.

When I was old enough to start school, I was smart and a quick learner, so the most trouble I had in the first grade was staying entertained. I had long, beautiful, thick hair and I'd sit in class and flop it over my face, remaining like that until the teacher noticed and told me to "take my hair out of my face." I would flop all of my hair back and giggle uncomfortably. I got a big laugh out of my classmates each time I did it too.

I see now it was a cry for help. This was my brave attempt at telling my teacher someone was hurting me. Instead, my teacher was frustrated by my poor behavior and handed me a note, which I gave to my mother. She was immediately enraged. "Are you flopping your hair in front of your face, MacKenzie?" I laughed uneasily as a response to her question, so she grabbed my wrist and a pair of scissors and forced me to sit in a chair.

Before I knew what was happening, she chopped my hair off. I was crying and whimpering like a wounded animal the whole time, devastated.

"You deserve this for being so bad in class!"

I stiffened and made sure to sit extra still so she wouldn't stab me with the scissors. I was frozen in sheer terror.

"Now you won't be able to flop your hair in front of your face!"

She chopped and cut and hacked my hair beyond its former recognition. Panicked, she then rushed me to a stylist, who permed my now short, thick hair. It finally represented a bush of sorts on top of my head.

I hid in my room in shame, crying and claiming I would never leave the house again. When I returned to school, I was called "bushwhacker" mercilessly by the other children until my hair grew out.

Fast forward to many years later, and my mother decided to go back to school to get her hairdresser license. Each and every single time I sat in her chair, I was terrified of her touching me. This mystified me. Why was I so scared of her doing my hair? For a long time, I thought that it was simply because she would never give me the hair style or color I desired; instead, she'd do whatever she wanted to do. Due to many buried traumatic childhood memories being inaccessible to me (as this one was for many years), I couldn't make the connection. Now, I see why my body remembered what my mind had lost.

By the time third grade rolled around (and my hair had grown back), my mother allowed us to get our first pet, a cat named Cuddles. She was feisty and had spent her first few years of life living outdoors in a rural area, but I loved her fighting spirit and immediately felt comforted by her purr. Cuddles was my only emotional support in my home.

I was literally a head taller than all of the other girls in my grade, so my father decided to sign me up for basketball and volunteered to coach as well. I had a knack for playing and picked up the game with ease. Very quickly, I became our team's leading scorer and rebounder.

When I stepped onto the basketball court, everything would go quiet, almost like time and the life I knew at home didn't exist. I left the chaos of my mind at the door and entered into an alternate reality where I could express myself and channel my emotions. The court was the one place where everything made sense to me: There were solid rules and regulations to abide by, and they never changed. I reveled in the ability to be embraced by a team of players who treated me like one of their own. For the first time, I belonged and was accepted. The court was the functioning, dependable, reliable family I had been longing to find.

The road to success I found in the realm of basketball was in stark contrast to life lived with my actual family. I didn't know what the rules were, since they were always changing, but regardless, I certainly always broke them and found myself on the receiving end of lectures, punishments, and being reminded that no matter how hard I tried to get along with everyone, I was not capable of achieving this.

My father was thrilled to see the talent I showed at an early age and quickly became a resource for unsolicited advice about how I could and should play the game. His approach frustrated me because he struggled to understand how I saw basketball: as the family I never had, as the acceptance I sought, as the mechanism through which I was learning about life. Basketball was more than points scored and rebounds; to me it was a parent, of sorts. The game was teaching me how to fall down and get back up, how to work with others, how to assert leadership skills, and how to handle stressful situations. His critiques of my performance and being graded according to statistics were hurtful because he neglected to ask what the game meant to me.

As an added bonus as I continued to excel on the basketball court, my parents were allowing me to miss church on Wednesday nights to attend practice. For the first time in memory, I was gaining some freedom from the oppression of church forced on me by my parents.

I truly loved Jesus and God, but the lives I saw churchgoers living never quite connected with the godly lifestyle they proclaimed, and that confused me. I spent a lot of time wondering what church was really all about and what I should be learning while I was there. I was seeing a lot of duplicity, and it felt fraudulent to me. Was church one great, big sham? I looked forward to the day when I could decide how to work out my own faith without compulsion.

Growing up, when I dared to challenge my mother about the treatment I was receiving, she would reply, "I treat you all equally. No one is treated differently."

This was her catch-all phrase, repeated on a loop, and is the one thing I remember her embedding in me that would override how she actually treated me. When I believed her lie that I was not being treated any differently from my siblings, I was the one in error for thinking how she treated me was wrong.

I know now, as a parent, it is impossible to treat my son, Lincoln, who is eleven, exactly the same as my daughter, Vada, who is five. Each child is unique and comes with his or her own personality and characteristics. If I claimed I treated them each the same, that would mean I wasn't acknowledging their uniqueness and labeling them as if they were not special in their own right of existence. Different children require different levels of care, compassion, kindness, and understanding.

My mother took away my ability to be heard – to feel special and valued for being an individual. By claiming equal treatment, she got to bulldoze past anything that was different about me and silence me in the process, without addressing any of my concerns. In doing so, she made me doubt my own feelings about how she treated me. Instead, I constantly pushed past my feelings and shoved them aside, in exchange for the lie that I was being treated equally, even though I knew it wasn't the case.

She left me no other choice. I thought it must be me doing something wrong and perceiving something wrong, but I couldn't figure out what.

As time progressed throughout my childhood, it became easier for me to accept the narrative my mother continually forced on me. I believed she knew me better than I knew myself.

CHAPTER 4

Born to Stand Out

I was playing basketball nearly year-round and had become friends with girls on my team as seventh grade approached. Life fell into a sort of rhythm for me, with basketball at the core. I had embraced the new family I found on the court. I worked very hard to hone my skills and enjoyed practicing. Word traveled quickly to family members about my performance on the court, and my grandfather and grandmother on my dad's side rarely missed a game. Although my father would pick up any shift at the factory offered to him, he never missed me playing, either. My mother constantly complained that her parents never made it to watch me play, despite her repeated invitations, and I could tell it really hurt her. Honestly, it hurt me too. As a result, instead of celebrating who did show up to support me, I focused on who wasn't there.

Looking forward, my father decided he didn't like the situation with the current high school coach: He wasn't winning many games, and Dad wanted me to be partnered with a winning program. A couple of towns over, there was a coach who had an established pattern of winning. My parents communicated we were moving, very matter-of-factly, to all of us. I had no say in the matter. The only stable, dependable, reliable family I had known up to that point was ripped out of my hands.

And worse, I felt like my sister and my brother blamed me for it. I could feel the contempt as they, too, were simultaneously torn from their school, their friends, their neighborhood. Yet again, they had been shown where to target their upset feelings and unleash their unprocessed emotions. The move was MacKenzie's fault.

I was left, as usual, holding the bag. I had no one to blame but myself, since it was apparent that I was the reason for everyone's lives being suddenly and violently uprooted. Before I knew what hit me, I was starting my eighth-grade year in a new town, in a new school, with new people and new coaches. Cell phones and social media weren't a thing back then, and my parents did not make sure I kept some semblance of normalcy from my past, so I lost all of my old teammates too.

Meanwhile, my parents made it abundantly clear to everyone the singular reason for our move was for me to have a better basketball coach in high school. The burden I carried got heavier: What if I couldn't live up to everyone's expectations on the court?

I decided to go out for the track team in eighth grade for the first time, and made it to state in the high jump. I was finding success in the realm of athletics at whatever I attempted, but I didn't feel the same way about my victories as I had before we moved.

The pressure felt like it was mounting, and with it, the basketball court started to transition from a place of safety, solace, and freedom to a confining, rigid place where I was expected to perform my very best every single game. I hardly recognized it when I'd head out to play. I missed how it used to feel, back when I enjoyed it and had fun with my former family of teammates. Now, it felt tainted, like everything else in my life.

With my safe space stripped of its former comforts, I was spinning. There was no place that I could rely on to ground me. And I was having more and more thoughts all the time about my biological father.

I would pull out the lone Polaroid picture my mother had given me when I was first told about his existence and ask him every single question that came to mind. "Who are you? Where are you? Why didn't you want me? Why did you leave me here? Are you coming to find me?" He'd stare back at me, seated in his chair, smoking a cigarette and say the same thing, every time: nothing.

He was just a mystery man in a picture, after all. He was a missing piece in the ongoing puzzle that could bring me stability and insight into my identity. It brought on immense pain when I did take the time to confront him and his existence and what that meant to me.

He looked around fifty years old in the picture, more like he should have been my grandpa. I had a hard time picturing this old smoker with my much younger mother. She made it clear that he had hurt her and was in the mafia, and that she did not want to discuss the details, whenever I dared to bring up the subject. However, she'd bring him up sporadically over the years on her own terms, to share ever-changing stories and new ones I'd never heard previously.

If I could never find him and never meet him, how would I know who I was? I pictured him finding me and would often think about him while I was out in public. "What if he's in this very room now?" I'd think and my heart would beat faster with anticipation at the thought. Did he ever think of me or wonder about me too?

The thought haunted me more and more, but I was entering my freshman year of high school and had to do my best to focus.

To everyone's surprise, I made the varsity volleyball team as a freshman. My family had focused entirely on my basketball skills to date, and I didn't quite comprehend at the time what an achievement this was; actually, in my mind, it was the opposite. I didn't get to play with my friends who were on the freshman team. Most of the upperclassman I played with didn't include me in their conversations, wouldn't willingly answer my questions, and treated me like an unwelcome intruder, stepping into a varsity team spot without paying my dues.

Soon I was in the starting lineup, which made me even more of a target – stealing a starting spot from an upperclassman! Parents of the other players were unhappy and felt slighted by the coach starting me over their daughter. I felt the anger and conflict.

Before gym, we changed out of our street clothes into uniforms comprised of shorts and T-shirts in a lofty room with high ceilings and supporting beams I could touch, if I jumped. After class, I'd return to find my padlock undone and my clothing draped over the beams. My bra, shirt, and pants were displayed in plain sight. I'd have to jump around to gather the various garments daily. I spent most my time in gym feeling anxious and dreading going back to the locker room to get changed. Worse, I knew whoever was bullying me was probably watching as I jumped to retrieve my garments.

Finally, one day, I'd had enough. I lagged behind after I changed and hid myself in a little nook in the door. I observed two cheerleaders dressed in their varsity uniforms unlocking my padlock. I recognized them as close friends of girls on my volleyball team. I snuck up behind them, cleared my throat loudly, and asked, "What do you think you're doing? I'm tired of jumping around to get my clothing every day." Their wide eyes and open mouths stared back at me in disbelief. They timidly agreed to my terms and muttered, "We will stop" and slinked away. No one touched my clothing again.

By sophomore year, I was playing, starting, and excelling at basketball, volleyball, and track. I played the center position in basketball and the middle front-row hitter in volleyball, and threw the discus, ran the four-hundred, and did high jump in track. I briefly attempted hurdles before I caught one during a race and it sent me face-first to the track. It was decided that wasn't my thing.

I was 6'1" tall by this point and trying to adjust to my height. I had a slender, muscular frame and I wore men's jeans because I couldn't find any women's clothing that fit me. I often wore my dad's sweaters and khakis when I had to dress up before basketball or volleyball games. I decided that I was going to rock, own, and love my height from the earliest that I can remember.

Thankfully, my mother, standing at 5'11" herself, had prior experience dealing with height. She always was proud to be tall and viewed being tall as a privilege. It was confusing to me that she supported a part of my identity as a positive attribute, but on the other hand, another part of it (my biological father), was viewed as shameful and too awful to formally address. As a result, I was always at war with my identity because "Mother knew best."

My parents placed a huge emphasis on obtaining a basketball scholarship, so they had rigid rules about not partying, and I was not allowed to stay the night at friends' houses. One night, after a football game, my friends and I went to a restaurant. My friends were wearing cheerleading and football uniforms. One of the players said it'd be cool if we all walked out on our bills, so I followed the group and left without paying. The restaurant knew who we were by the uniforms, of course, and we were called in one-by-one and questioned.

I decided honesty to be the best policy, so I openly confessed to the dean at my school. It turned out I was the only one who did, and as a result, they suspended me for part of the volleyball season my sophomore year. No one else was punished.

I went back and paid my meager bill at the restaurant. But it sat sourly with me that while I did make a foolish choice originally, I admitted my mistake and got punished while others lied and remained free to play their sport.

I learned that simply following the crowd wasn't for me. Truth be told, I always stood out. Whenever I tried to blend in, it didn't go well. Case in point: Even if you messed up and admitted it when no one else would, what did that get you besides punished, while everyone else lied and got away scot-free?

For the first time, I was starting to think about what justice means. This experience showed me that even adults don't always do the right thing. I stood by my decision and decided regardless of what other people did, I would do my best to be honest, even if it meant standing on my own.

CHAPTER 5

God, *The Matrix*, and Destiny

I have always been obsessed with watching movies, for as long as I can remember, especially in the comfort of a theater with a large tub of popcorn and a giant soda. I even worked at one when I was in high school, so I could enjoy the perks of watching the newest releases for free.

When *The Matrix* was released into theatres in 1999, I was a junior in high school. In regards to my spiritual journey, I knew and believed God was real, perfect, awesome, and amazing, but there was one problem: I wasn't any of these things. Due to my family's treatment, and the fact that my biological father ditched me before I was born, I felt pretty worthless – like God didn't have much interest in me. And through my rigid and confusing time spent against my will in the Pentecostal church, I was very skeptical of our modern-day version of "church" as a whole.

I kept my beliefs to myself. I was leery of anyone who talked about God, simply because I'd been hurt by people claiming to believe in Him my whole life. As I watched Keanu Reeves play the role of Neo in the theater that day, I felt more truth downloaded into my soul than the entirety of the time I had spent going to church.

Something inside me had shifted and I started on a path to answer big questions: What is truth? What degree do we invest in this world and its systems, and to what extent does it distract us from who we really are meant to be? What is my destiny? What is my purpose?

I bought *The Matrix* on videotape and watched it repeatedly.

Meanwhile, I stopped playing volleyball, but continued with basketball and track through my senior year of high school. I hadn't dated anyone seriously until I met Damion, who became my first serious boyfriend. He went to a different high school, but met my stringent height requirements (must be taller than me, which turned out to be a "tall" order to fill).

As first loves do, we decided we'd be together forever, and we'd cement the deal by losing our virginity together. I wish I could say it was romantic, but I had just finished playing a basketball game and was still sweaty and in my uniform when we had sex for the first time.

Soon after, I noticed a large amount of excess tissue that hadn't been there before our encounter. In shock, I started crying and proclaiming, "I must be pregnant!"

Let me back up a bit and describe my sexual education to this point: Don't have sex. That was about it. My parents did not have a single talk with me about sex, about what it is, about what you do, about how to protect yourself, nothing. Pretty much all the information I gathered about sex was from friends who had already done it, biology class, and my own assumptions.

Horrified, I went to my mother with this information and we went to my first gynecologist appointment. As usual, there was no preparation or helpful conversation from my mother to warn me what was coming. They put my legs up in stirrups, inspected the tissue, and proceeded to numb me and operate on the spot.

I was melting down and doing my best to stay still, completely freaked out by what was happening. My mother had opted to stay outside. I was alone and terrified. When I was allowed to sit up, there was blood everywhere, all over the white paper underneath me. The gynecologist left the room suddenly, and I was alone, wondering where everyone went and what was happening. Why was the doctor so silent and freaked out? Something was wrong.

My mother walked in the room and grabbed me, and we walked outside to her car. As soon as I was seated and buckled in, with wide eyes,

I looked at her mulling over how to put what had just happened into words.

Before I could speak, she said, "The gynecologist said that the type of tissue damage she removed was consistent with girls who have been molested. I know it was your father. He must have done it when you were a baby, and that's why you probably don't remember."

At the time of this incident, she had decided she was going to file for divorce from Paul. My mother neglected to ask me what happened, how I felt, or even if I was okay.

I was in a state of twofold shock. First, shock about the sexual abuse, then, secondly, shock about her accusation. My father never acted inappropriately with me, but because she had gaslit me my whole life (unbeknownst to me at the time), I questioned my own reality constantly and was unsure about my own experiences unless she validated them. The blow of her allegations knocked the wind out of my mental sails, combined with the trauma I had endured already to this point – and I completely bypassed the fact that I was actually sexually abused and never made the connection to my former neighbor.

Anything related to the operation I had just endured was erased. It was like I somehow turned it off and put it with all the other things I'd had to turn off over the years to survive.

Maybe it was God's way of protecting me until we had a good relationship, so I could properly process and heal from all the trauma. Truthfully, dumping the memories more than likely saved my life.

I'd often fantasize in my free time about what it would be like if I wasn't here anymore, and this very possibly could have put me over the edge. I never attempted anything, but I liked to entertain the idea that death meant no more pain – and wondered what it would feel like to be free.

My mother never asked me a question about the incident. She never offered to get me a counselor, or any kind of professional help. Instead, she told me she knew it was my father because "he'd always been a pervert." She assumed she already knew what happened to me, allocated the blame where she wanted, and declared herself the ultimate authority over me, my life, and my experiences, yet again.

My mother knew from this experience that I was sexually active, but she didn't speak with me about that, either. We never discussed safe sex and condoms or birth control or any pregnancy-prevention measures.

With literally no memory of everything that had just occurred, I continued to navigate my senior year of high school. I was named "Player of the Year" by the local news station, and I made the Illinois All-State team for basketball. My high school peers voted me "Most Athletic" and "Best Legs" and I had maintained decent grades. Pretty much everyone in my town knew who I was, due to my athletic ability, and this never ceased to make me feel uncomfortable. I smiled and was polite but didn't particularly enjoy being so easily recognizable.

But then again, I was unusually tall and realized that simply leaving town didn't mean I'd stop being noticed. I was a successful, popular, accomplished athlete who was mounting up achievements and recognitions with a bright future ahead.

Next, I received a basketball scholarship from Illinois Central College. They were many-times over NJCAA champions and had a coach noted for decades of winning. I felt honored to have the privilege to play for Lorene Ramsey and accepted the offer excitedly. However, it also meant I would stay at home due to the short commute.

During my freshman year at ICC, I ended the season as the leading scorer and rebounder on my team. I was making straight A's, exceling on the court, making lots of friends, and enjoying college life, but I noticed there was this pretty constant feeling that I was forgetting something. More like a hazy cloud in my mind and a feeling that something was wrong that I struggled to shake.

I attributed it to the lingering question of my paternity. Why couldn't I just get over it? I guess I would always wonder about him.

But each time I considered the possibility of going to find him, terror would strike. My mother's words haunted me: "If you ever do try to find him, he will surely kill me, and possibly you." I felt constantly conflicted about what action, if any, I could take to conquer this nagging feeling, this pit in my stomach that made me feel uneasy in my own skin. My hands were tied by my mother's threats. I felt helpless to pursue my desire to connect with him. When I went out with my friends and danced and drank, I noticed the pit would dissolve. Distraction was becoming my closest friend.

Distraction also came in the form of a cute boy from philosophy class, whom I met after Damion and I ended our relationship. Mathias was studying to become a pastor, and his vocation of choice perked my interest and fascinated me. Maybe he could offer me a new perspective on church and God, something I hadn't considered previously.

I believed in God and Jesus, but I still liked to go out and party with my friends on the basketball team, and as our relationship continued, this was a problem. He made it clear he did not approve of alcohol at all, ever, under no condition, but I felt differently and continued to live my life despite his disapprovals. We fought about my clothing being "too tight" or "too revealing," and as time went on, his demands became more and more rigorous and controlling. We fought constantly over our differences and our relationship continued to deteriorate from there; neither of us was willing to budge or compromise, but we were still very much invested in our relationship.

In addition, my mother sat me down in our living room and told me she was leaving my father, after twenty-plus years of marriage. "I never loved your father. Only tolerated him. And I always said that when you kids were grown up enough, I was going to leave him. Now you are grown, and I am leaving."

The words rolled off her tongue so callously and matter-of-factly that I shuddered. I felt like the little girl again, sitting at the kitchen table. Another man was walking out of my life. And my mother neglected to assemble our whole family for any kind of conversation about the divorce.

Very shortly after her announcement, she began seeing another man. My family had to live together in the same home, with two parents going through a divorce because neither was financially stable enough. You could cut the tension with a knife. I did anything to avoid being at home, like spending the nights at Mathias' or at a friend's house. It didn't really matter, as long as I wasn't at home because the thought of yet another man leaving my life was more than I could take.

I was crushed their marriage was over. My mom had moved on so quickly.

I spiraled with news of the divorce – and partied, partied, partied with my friends, whenever I got the chance. By my sophomore year, I was barely attending class, but still pulling some decent grades. I went from being mostly a straight-A student to a couple of B's, mostly C's, and a D. My coaches were noticing, and I had also gotten quite the reputation as a party girl.

Halfway through my sophomore year, I was suddenly benched. I had never sat on the bench for any amount of time in my athletic career. Now, even basketball – my home, my family, my parent, the only place I felt I could look to for stability – was rejecting me.

No matter how hard I played, or how hard I tried, if I did get put in a game, it was for five minutes. I was devastated and humiliated by this. The coaching staff attributed my benching to my poor defense and slipping grades. I was still passing some classes, but my grades had definitely dropped.

In the throes of a nasty divorce with my parents, being benched, and my quickly deteriorating relationship with Mathias, I was coming apart at the seams.

I did receive several Division One scholarship offers to play, and my coach wanted me to sign with the University of Texas at El Paso (UTEP). She thought the best thing I could do was get away from my house and the town with everything going on, and looking back, she was probably right. But due to being benched, I had lost all of my confidence in my ability to play basketball and had no desire to continue.

Sadly, I devastated my dad by turning down the lucrative Division One scholarship offers. He had moved out of our home, and just as quickly, my mother had moved a new man into our home, as well as his adult son and their large dog. She would later marry him, and he became my stepfather. Of course, there was never a conversation where she asked how I felt about this sudden shift.

It sent me over the edge, her changing out my father role, yet again without so much as a conversation. Worse, the timing coincided with my sudden benching my sophomore year of college.

I was devastated. How could my mother do this to me? Her decision destroyed my relationship with basketball. I lost faith in my ability to play at the next level. I felt lost and devastated, but simultaneously there was an unexplainable knowing that grounded me and prevented me from spinning out of control despite all logic to the contrary.

Somehow, everything was going to be okay.

CHAPTER 6

Cuddles

I spent as many nights away from home and at my boyfriend's house as possible. I managed to stay away for weeks at a time. When I would return to the house, I'd always look for my comfort cat, Cuddles.

By this time, she was elderly. She'd always been an indoor/outdoor cat, but had never coexisted with dogs, and I'm sure she was beyond frightened of the new German shepherd suddenly living in our home. After searching frantically for her, I was saddened when my mom told me she hadn't seen her in weeks.

Her absence only compounded my heartbreak and left me feeling even more desolate and depressed. Heaving heavy sobs, I prayed and asked God to help me find Cuddles. I drifted off to sleep exhausted, and suddenly, I was transported to another reality.

I'd had dreams before this night, but nothing that felt like I was actually living inside the scope of the dream. In this dream, I woke up, found myself in my bedroom in my mom's house, stretched, and saw the sunlight coming in through the windows. Still half asleep, I got out of bed, walked down the stairs, and through the kitchen to the back porch, where my mom had a fresh pot of coffee brewing. I grabbed a white mug and poured myself a cup. I peeked outside. My mother was seated at the table on our red-orange deck. The trees in the ravine provided a picturesque backdrop to the beautiful, sunny morning. I met my mother's gaze and walked out to meet her on the deck, coffee in hand.

"Mom," I said. "I just had the most realistic dream, and it happened exactly the same way as it is happening now."

Intrigued, I walked over to the trees in the ravine. Bending over the railing on the deck, I called as loudly as I could: "Here kitty, kitty, kitty ... Cuddles!"

Suddenly, Cuddles came running out of the ravine, full force, her tail in the air. I was reunited with my lost companion.

Then I woke up.

I was devastated to discover that I had not been reunited with my cat, that it had not been real, and struggled to sort out how I could have just experienced a dream that felt more like a memory – something I'd already lived, somehow. Eerily, as I took in my surroundings, I noticed the sun peeking through my blinds the exact same way.

I stretched, got out of bed, and walked down the stairs and through the kitchen to the coffee brewing. I grabbed a white coffee mug to help myself to a cup. All this was really starting to internally freak me out a bit.

"If my mom is sitting outside right now..." I thought to myself, peering out to check.

And there she was, seated on the deck.

I went outside. The air was fresh and crisp and I was getting excited. I greeted my mom and said, "I just had this dream and everything was exactly like this, you sitting on the deck, the coffee brewing ... and then I went to call for Cuddles over by the ravine, and she came running."

My mom looked very skeptical, but before she spoke, I walked to the rail of the deck and yelled as loud as I could: "Here kitty, kitty, kitty ... Cuddles!"

Suddenly, she was racing toward me, out of the foliage, straight into my arms! I could not believe my dream had just come to pass in front of my very eyes, and we were reunited in real life.

That was the last time I ever saw Cuddles alive, thanks to an answered prayer.

Mathias ended our relationship after my father denied his request to marry me, and I now resided full-time with my mother, her boyfriend, his son, my sister, and my brother. I was waitressing and tension was high in my home.

My mother wanted me gone. She used the excuse that I wasn't keeping my room clean enough. I found an apartment running a $99 move-in promotion rate for the first month. I had that money, but not much else, and no idea how I was going to make the $599 monthly rent going forward, not to mention utilities and everything else, like furniture and food. I felt robbed of a cheery transition. There was no help from my mother with moving, furniture, or any necessities. She cut off all contact with me.

It was the dead of winter in central Illinois and fresh snow had just fallen onto the ground. My father showed up in his shiny red truck, ready to help me move out of the house that he and my mother once shared. Now divorced from my mother and out on his own, I greatly appreciated his help because no one else offered.

The only furniture I had to move into my apartment was my bed. My mother wouldn't let me take anything else. My transition to independence was a monumental moment in my life that should have been celebrated; yet here it was, scary and shocking. I truthfully had no idea how I was going to make it – financially, emotionally, or otherwise – but that didn't seem to concern my mother in the least. I was her daughter, yet I felt like she did not care what happened to me one way or another.

We loaded the bed into my father's truck, lightly secured it, and started to make our way on the windy, blustering, cold day. I followed behind him on the small, two-lane road in my 1991 Eagle Talon with the rest of my belongings.

Suddenly, a huge gust of wind caught the bed in my dad's trunk, lifted it, and hoisted it out into the snow. Another vehicle ran over it. I watched in horror as my only piece of furniture occupied a snowy lane.

My father and I pulled over to assess the damage. The mattress was covered in sludgy snow. Springs popped out of the blue, floral pattern.

"Okay," my dad said. "I have an idea. You drive my truck and we'll load this in the back. The mattress is still salvageable, so I'll just climb on top of it and hold it down with my body weight so it doesn't go anywhere while you drive."

I admired that he was willing to go to such lengths to help me out, but the fact that my only possession was in shambles was starting to register.

He mounted the mattress, his face red and blustery from the strong wind and low temperatures. Pulling away from the side of the road and into traffic, I fixed my eyes on the rearview mirror. I could only see his head and his mouth moving, accompanying a faint "SLOOOOW DOWNNN." I could see he was trying with all his might to grip the mattress. Tears rolled down my cheeks as I realized my father might fly off and into traffic. Simultaneously, I was holding back laughter. It felt like a scene from a movie, only this was my life. This was real life.

Before I could think another thought, I heard sirens behind me. As the cop got out of his car and approached us, he observed my dad's spread-eagle position trying to hold onto the dirty, soiled mattress with springs popping out of it. He shook his head in disbelief and an amused smile creeped across his face.

"Ma'am, um, I'm not sure what's going on here, but he can't be, um, doing what he's doing."

He was kind and entertained but perplexed, and let us go with a warning. My dad gave me his own bed to sleep on, took me to Dollar General, and bought me some necessities.

I drank and partied most nights with work friends, when I wasn't waitressing double shifts to pay my rent. Between keeping occupied with work and partying, I had found enough to distract me from all the loose ends lingering in my life. I did my best to shove my feelings down regarding my mother's treatment and to carry on and survive on my own.

I was struggling, but still making my rent payment each month. Soon, I was introduced to Griffin, a friend of a friend.

He was tall and a bit of hippie, laughed easily, and was my age. He didn't have any real goals or ambitions, and at that point, neither did I. I enjoyed being around him, with his easygoing personality, and we started to date.

Soon we were together constantly. Griffin still lived at home, and some nights I would stay with him, but most nights were spent in my apartment.

One hungover morning, I went to grab my rainbow macramé woven wallet, where I kept my rent money, which was due that day. I looked in every nook and cranny for my woven wallet, but it was nowhere to be found.

My mother wasn't speaking to me, but out of desperation, I called her and pleaded with her for help. She accused me of making the whole story up and refused, even though she had not helped me with anything the entire time I'd been living on my own. My electricity was shut off soon after, and I was living without power, taking cold showers, and trying to figure out how to survive. Quickly, an eviction notice appeared on my door.

Again, I called my mother, and this time I asked her if she would let me move back home. Without hesitation, she shot me down: "No way. Absolutely not. You are not welcome in this house. You left, now you figure it out."

Even being forced out of my own home was my fault.

I collapsed in a puddle of tears under the weight of her words. I couldn't figure out what I'd done that was so terrible I wouldn't be welcomed in my own home. How could she not see that it was her actions that continually drove me away? Her lack of caring or concern for me and my feelings, her inability to have a conversation about anything that impacted me, her callous, harsh demeanor. True to form, when I needed her the most, she turned her back on me and kicked me while I was down.

I had no money, no electricity, and nowhere to go. I embraced the things I had no control over and decided to celebrate by throwing candle parties in my apartment. I was still alive and breathing, and I had tried my hardest to make it on my own. My friends brought over battery-operated radios and we celebrated life.

One day I returned home to find my key no longer worked. All my possessions had been seized, and I was officially homeless.

I temporarily crashed on a friend's futon and called my dad. He was living in a home in a town nearby and offered to let me move in with him. Looking back, I see now my father has been the one to step in and offer support, even though my mother had manipulated me into believing it was the other way around.

I moved all of my belongings to my dad's residence and settled into the basement.

One morning at Griffin's house, I noticed a queasiness. I'd felt seasick for a few days. I had brushed it off initially as maybe I'd eaten something bad, but now I worried it may be something more. Griffin bought a pregnancy test and I took it in his bathroom. The seconds felt like hours as I watched the test and waited for it to change color.

Finally, the results surfaced. I grabbed the test, rushed out of the bathroom, and flew outside to meet Griffin in the driveway. I kicked the white pebbled rocks that formed his driveway while wracking my mind for the words.

"I'm pregnant."

Speaking them out loud for the first time made everything feel more real and solidified.

We broke the news to Griffin's parents, who were very kind to me. They wanted us to put the baby up for adoption and even knew a couple personally who were struggling to have their own children. They offered to arrange a meeting.

The mention of the word "adoption" made me recoil. I was technically half-adopted myself, and it had haunted me my whole life – not knowing who that other person was, where they were. I made many assumptions about adoption strictly based on my own personal life experiences. I knew what it felt like to not know half of my biology. How could I do that to this child, with BOTH parents? How could I put my own child through twice the misery I'd gone through?

Her adoptive parents would remind her that she was a bad girl when she did something wrong because she came from bad people. They would refuse to talk to her about where she came from, or answer any of her questions, and put her in her room for hours at a time to cry unattended, until beaten down and broken she would stop trying to ask the questions that burned in her soul twenty-four hours a day. She would give up and decide that her parents must be right and accept there was something wrong with her, something forever different and broken that everyone else saw so clearly, except her.

She would never be able to figure out what she had done to be treated this way, only accept that she deserved it, or it wouldn't be happening.

Adoption was something to be ashamed of. Something people used as a reason to treat you as less of a person.

Again, I made the decision to reach out to my mother. She doubled down and told me I could not move back into the home, yet again. She also suggested that I give up my baby for adoption.

It crushed me. She had never taken the time to understand what not knowing my biological father had been like, or had the conversations with me I needed to have, and here she was carelessly suggesting I do the same thing to my own child.

I wanted to throw up. Not just because I was so sick all the time during the pregnancy, but because I felt like I didn't matter to her. She had decided adoption was the best thing for my baby, not stopping to think about what I needed or wanted. She never asked me, just reminded me, "You're on your own."

CHAPTER 7

My Choice

My relationship with Griffin was breaking down. We'd looked at an apartment together, but he did not have a job, and I couldn't make the rent each month on my own. He was around less and less, and I think the stress about being a father was getting to him. He stayed out partying all night while I laid awake trying to figure out how I was going to raise this baby.

The truth of his absence was hitting me hard: I could not raise my baby without a father. I'd never known my own biological father, the pain I felt was overwhelming, and I'd never mastered how to deal with it. How was I going to walk her through something I didn't know how to deal with myself? How could I have my baby knowing I was going to put her through the same torment?

I scheduled a visit to learn what kind of government assistance would be available to me. I was assigned a case worker. The details were varied and overwhelming, and the housing I qualified for was in a very poor part of town, so poor I would be concerned for my safety and my child's safety. And who would watch my baby while I went to work?

I was willing to keep my baby, but I felt like my hands were tied. How could I make this work with no support, no experience, no father to help me raise her? The facts were stacking up against me, and on top of that, I severely doubted my own capabilities to provide my child with the life she deserved. The thoughts and questions cycled through my head like a cyclone. There were no easy answers.

Finally, I went to my dad and told him about my pregnancy. I could tell he was in shock and struggled to know what to really say. He offered his help, but I knew he didn't know a lot about what to do with a baby because that was always my mom's department. I did not have the slightest clue how to change a diaper or feed a baby and felt completely overwhelmed.

My father was the only one who had stepped up and offered, but I knew the kind of help he was offering was not the kind I needed. I needed my mother. I NEEDED her. Why wasn't she helping me? Why wouldn't she listen to me? She had wiped her hands clean of me and was concerned only with herself and her new relationship with my stepdad. She had never listened to me in the past; why did I expect now to be so different? I was in dire need of her help and guidance to raise this baby, to be a shoulder to cry on, but she was not there. I cried and cried for my mother.

I was breaking down. I'd come to a point in my life where everything I'd avoided and tried not to think about was surfacing and confronting me head on. I was trying to figure out the best options for me and my baby based on my own life experiences and had no one to speak with about the options on the table. I felt ashamed, embarrassed, stupid, and angry. I was angry that I was the one left to decide someone else's life when I couldn't even figure out my own.

In addition to all the unresolved issues I had regarding my own identity, I was also trying to make this decision under the most duress I'd ever been in, and feeling very ill from the pregnancy. I was in a state of constant shock with the depths of my situation never fully settling. I sank into deep depression over the decision that had to be made.

There was one remaining option that I had not dared to consider.

My strict church upbringing made it blaringly obvious where I would go if I ever even considered … I couldn't even think it. My self-doubt and self-worth were at an ultimate low and I felt like the scum of the earth even thinking about thinking about it.

Abortion.

The truth had become blaringly obvious. I didn't possess the capabilities mentally, emotionally, or financially to keep this baby. I could not give her up for adoption and resign her to the abusive, tormented, confusing, painful existence I had endured. I was terrified of making the wrong decision, but I had no idea what was right – they were each wrong, for various reasons.

I was making one of the biggest decisions of my life with very little support and a combination of unprocessed, repressed, unrecognized memories of sexual, emotional, mental, and physical abuse.

I stopped taking my prenatal pills and called the Abortion Clinic to schedule an appointment. I disgusted myself at the thought of what I was going to do and wondered how I'd even be able to look at myself in the mirror again. I beat myself up constantly until the date of my appointment arrived.

A friend picked me up. As we arrived at the clinic, we were met with protestors. "Baby Killer!" and "Murderer!" rang out from their lips. I felt even more judged, even more unredeemable.

I wondered if they had any idea that I wanted to keep my baby, but had no means to do so. I wondered if any of the protestors actually had a solution to offer someone like me, rather than calling me names I'd already called myself. I wondered what they thought about the man who'd gotten me pregnant, and why they weren't picketing in front of his house.

Here I was, about to do the very thing to my unborn child that my biological father wanted to do to me. I felt sickened by the situation and the protesters were salt in my wounds, adding to the pain.

The clinic was gray inside. It felt cold and sterile. I was handed a questionnaire asking me things like how many abortions I'd had prior to this one. I handed the clipboard back to the receptionist and was led into a room. I changed into a gown. A woman placed cold gel on my stomach and performed a sonogram. I leaned over to see the picture on the screen, but she covered it, so I wasn't able to see my baby.

A cold chill went down my spine. Reality hit me in that moment. I was only a couple of months along, but this baby was real, as confirmed by the sonogram.

They escorted me out of the room. I kept trying to talk myself into going through with it, reassuring myself I'd be able to put it all behind me soon.

But everything inside me was screaming: "GET UP AND LEAVE!"

I thought it was just nerves, but this voice was louder and clearer than I had ever heard.

"GET UP AND LEAVE!"

The voice shook me, but I was led into another room full of women in hospital gowns. Each of them was distraught, some weeping silently, some loudly, some staring forward, expressionless, as if they were numb. I glanced from face to face, noting how we were all in the same situation.

"GET UP AND LEAVE!"

The voice again. This time I searched the other expressions intently, expecting one of the other women to meet my gaze and say, "I heard it too."

That didn't happen.

Next, someone called my name. As we were walking to the procedure room, she said, "You're in luck. We have a doctor with us today from Milwaukee who will be performing your abortion. He's really good."

Tears welled in my eyes. Milwaukee.

The place where I was conceived.

The pill they gave me started to take effect. But I could not believe the sickening coincidence. I couldn't get over the fact that Milwaukee had come for my baby.

As I drowsily found my bearings in the recovery room, I was told the procedure went well. I could grab my things and go.

But Milwaukee was the nail in my spiritual coffin.

"I'm officially going to hell," I thought. "If I had any question about it before, now I don't. I'm unredeemable."

My mom had called it from the start. I was bad. I was not worthy of love or attention or any explanations. She knew with one look that I was trouble. And she was right. I was an angry baby. All along. I just deserved pain and misery and loss.

I needed to just figure out now how to live in the moment. Not dwell on my past. Make the most out of my life. My abortion would not be in vain. I promised that I was going to make something out of my life, for *her*.

If it had not been for this pregnancy, I don't know if I would have ever seriously considered my future. I couldn't depend on a guy to do things for me, or my mother. Somehow, I needed to do better moving forward independently. This became my new focus.

My good friend was waiting for me outside the clinic. She drove us to her house and I rested on her futon. I felt very uncomfortable cramping, but the nauseous feeling that had plagued me during my pregnancy was noticeably absent. I missed it.

The events from the clinic were flashing through my memories like a horror film highlight reel. I was trying to comprehend what had just happened. I felt somehow detached from the whole experience and was having a hard time reconciling the events of the day as actual reality. I felt like I was watching someone else go through it.

The decision I'd made now crushed me with its finality. I was full of regret. When I wrote about the abortion in my diary, I chose to say simply, "Something was stolen from me."

I honestly believed all of this would go away once the abortion was finalized. Now, instead, I was only further propelled into a deeper place of sadness and loss. I believed the abortion to be a "procedure," but this felt like so much more. At times, flashes of grief hit me like a storm and completely overwhelmed me.

And it was a silent loss. I found it did not have a conversation or place with anyone. I was grieving alone and in a constant state of confusion and shock. It was a permanent choice and I had to deal with its ramifications and consequences for the rest of my life.

I'd have to figure out how to carry the loss with me. Why didn't anyone tell me it'd be like this afterwards? I felt so deceived by the lie that abortion had sold me: a way out of my circumstances and a way out of the pain.

No one mentioned the torturous emotional implications that I would have to endure. How did anyone else live like this? No one talks about this after an abortion.

Maybe I was the only one who regretted doing this? Maybe there were those out there that had abortions and felt completely fine afterwards?

Surely there had to be more women out there like me: hoping for a solution and a way out of an impossible circumstance, but instead finding themselves in a new, deeper level of pain and incomprehensible loss. Even if I had the courage to confess that I had an abortion and regretted it, would I find a shoulder to cry on? Would I find someone willing to look past the horrible stigma that a woman who has an abortion must bear in our society? Someone who would try to understand and sympathize with my pain?

At first, I told my mother and sister I had a miscarriage. I was so ashamed of my decision to abort that I couldn't even say the words out loud. As I began to process what happened, I later told them the truth about how I didn't feel I had any other options at the time, and had made the decision to abort.

At the time, my mother didn't apologize for turning her back on me when I needed help. This never registered as unkind to me – after all, that was just Mom. She could do and say anything to me, and it was excused because she had "good reasons" to treat me poorly. I had to remain silent. I didn't deserve to be heard.

I was still working at Applebee's during all this and had gotten my sister a job there as well, but when a robbery happened and four of my coworkers were trapped in a cooler by the assailants, I was shaken. They had taken one of my coworkers and shot him outside the cooler, leaving his dead body in front of it.

I couldn't not see his body when I attempted to go back to work after the incident. I knew I needed a new job, so I interviewed at Buffalo Wild Wings, a new restaurant concept in our area, and was hired on the spot. When I left the interview with a job that day, I had no idea I had just met my future husband.

CHAPTER 8

Healing, Love, and School

Brett was my manager at the time, and we started dating almost immediately. I recommended to him that we hire my sister, Ivy, so she could benefit as well. He was hesitant at first, but I was insistent because I wanted my sister to have a better income. The restaurant was very successful and packed night after night, and I was making the best money I'd ever made as a server. I was still living at my dad's so I was able to save some money.

My dad started dating someone in Tennessee and decided to move to be with her. When he left, I moved my best friend into the house. Ivy and her fiancée at the time decided they wanted to move in, so we all four lived in the house together. Due to the sibling dynamic my sister and I have – her the bully and me the silent one who didn't deserve a voice – she pushed me out of the way almost immediately and asserted her dominance over the residence.

She made several phone calls to my father, who was no longer in the area, pleading her case that I was not fit to remain in the home. As a result, I was told to vacate the premises.

My best friend and I decided to move into an apartment together and left the house. Soon after, my sister and her fiancée broke off their engagement and parted ways. Even though I was no longer living with my sister, we were still working together. She got Brett's phone number and, in an attempt to break us up, called him to share some of my negative narrative that she felt he needed to know. It wasn't enough for her to kick me out of the home we shared, now she needed to end my relationship as well.

Her attempt backfired and only served to show Brett what I had been up against my entire life: my sister's relentless attempts to destroy me and anyone who loved me. Altercations ensued at work. Brett took us outside in the middle of a shift to tell us both he needed us to get along on the restaurant floor. I rolled my eyes and said, "Okay, fine," and headed back inside the restaurant. My sister did the same but stopped in her tracks, with the door half open, and turned to Brett over her shoulder. "Just so you know, my sister is a liar. And she always has been a liar."

I did my best to excuse my sister's behavior because I had been told my entire life simply "to get along with her." So, I struggled to Scotch tape our relationship back together after each altercation. Ivy did not apologize for her behavior or claim any wrongdoing, so it was understood that I was the apologizer. I apologized right and left to her, and to my mother, for the entirety of my life, owning my own wrongs and taking on theirs as well because it was simply my role as the family scapegoat.

I desperately wanted to be close with my sister, but at each attempt, with each new job opportunity I gifted her, I was thwarted and treated worse. The more I laid down and let her stomp on me, the more liberties she took.

There wasn't a day that passed that I didn't think about my abortion. The memory haunted me, much like my biological father. I hated myself for making that decision and secretly mourned the loss of a child I'd never get to know, by my own actions. Guilt consumed me and rained in my soul like a perpetual storm.

I was tormented even further regarding my identity and my character since the abortion. What did God think of me now? Could He even look at me?

I felt like both the victim and perpetrator simultaneously. Sometimes I'd feel sorry for myself, how I was backed into a corner and forced to decide; other times I'd feel like a vicious monster, but the effect was always the same: shame, guilt, regret, anger, sadness, desperation, and a deep desire for rest and relief.

HEALING, LOVE, AND SCHOOL

Rest evaded me. I believed abortion would end the torment of "what do I do?" Instead, a new torment only took its place, hunting me daily. "How could you? You're a murderer! That was your baby! You're going to burn in hell!"

The words would hiss and linger and stay with me, badgering me, reminding me I was no good. There was no way to undo what had been done, but I desperately wanted to go back now and make a different choice. The memories of the clinic replayed in an endless loop, taunting me with the finality of my choice. I wondered what she would have looked like and who she would have been.

I'd just have to figure out a way to live in my new condition, but the pain I felt was agonizing. I truly believed up to that point that no one could save me, not even God. He didn't love me like He loved everyone else because I'd done too many bad things. I'd had an abortion, even, and no one gets to come back from that ultimate sin.

My mom handed me my first adult Bible on my thirteenth birthday, Sept. 23, 1993. It is a beautiful, maroon, leather-bound Bible with "MacKenzie Kay" inscribed in gold on the outside, along with my favorite Bible verse as a child.

We had moved numerous times growing up, and then I bounced around to a few apartments in my twenties. I lost many mementos in those moves, but this Bible had survived through it all. I marveled at how this book had made the journey. I couldn't specifically remember thinking I had to take it with me at any point, yet here it was, in my hands.

But what were the eternal ramifications of the consequences for the decisions I had made on Earth?

I stared at the verse, Romans 6:23, inscribed on my Bible as I pondered these questions deeply for the first time since my abortion. The book was stiff, still practically new at this point. I opened to find the corresponding scripture.

"For the wages of sin is death, but the free gift of God is eternal life through Christ Jesus our Lord." (The Living Bible Translation)

Suddenly the words had life and I understood in that moment what I hadn't thought possible before: There was hope for me yet.

"Listen to the words, MacKenzie. You are never too far gone."

I heard it like a gentle breeze, refreshing me.

"Could it really be true?" I thought, as tears formed in my eyes and I sobbed, right there, on Brett's sectional. I felt real hope for the first time in my life. I read and re-read this scripture, knowing with concrete certainty that I wasn't too far gone for God. I was never too far gone.

I rejoiced as the very Bible verse I had picked out all those years ago now provided renewed hope for me, and a fresh perspective. This moment was a huge shift for me in terms of my identity. For the first time, the light crept in and I knew I wasn't who I thought I was: a murderer, lacking, angry, bad blood, forsaken, too this or too that. People's opinions and labels could no longer define me. God found me and He defined me; nothing else, only love.

I could not earn what had already been done, and there was no level I had to get to first. It had been mine all along. I felt a shift in my spirit as the words planted in my soul and took root. Where did I get the idea that I had sinned too much, too wrongly, or too deeply to ever be forgiven? That I was unforgiveable? Religion dictated and insinuated standards and criteria needed to be met to be accepted by God, and I was found lacking. I never wavered in my belief in Him, but never understood that I was accepted just as I am in this very moment. **It was people's definition of God that made me feel I was never good enough or too far gone, not God himself.**

When I selected the verse as a little girl, I had no way of knowing it'd be this exact same verse, ten years later, that would bring freedom for me to start on a better path forward.

I started working a full-time job during the day. First as a temp without benefits, but then I was hired full-time through the company. I was awarded more pay per hour, medical benefits, and a 401k in the Ocean Export business.

Soon I got my roommate hired, and then, again, my sister. No matter how she treated me, I was like a puppy beaten by its owner that just wanted love and acceptance. Getting her a position at the company I worked for seemed like the best way to show her my undying loyalty.

I was four credits shy of my associate's degree and my roommate had decided to pursue her master's degree. She encouraged me to take advantage of the program the company was offering to pay for some schooling, and I remembered the promise I'd made after my abortion. I couldn't go back and undo what had been done, but I could focus on buckling down and pursuing my dreams.

I enrolled in Midstate College, where I attended evening classes that coordinated with my full-time job. I was also bartending and waitressing on the weekends, in addition to taking a full-time class schedule. I was constantly working and studying. I was tired, but I knew that without my bachelor's degree, I'd be limited in my professional career for the rest of my life.

I remained focused on my goals and within a few years, I had earned my bachelor's degree in business administration and graduated at the top of my class with honors, *magna cum laude*, with a 3.9 GPA. Simultaneously, I was engaged to marry Brett, and soon to be his wife, celebrating with my bachelorette party the same weekend as my graduation ceremony.

I was twenty-seven years old and it was one of the most exciting weekends of my life. I felt like all of my hard work was paying off, and I was excited to marry Brett, the love of my life.

My dad was now living in Tennessee and had married my stepmother. They invited my brother to move in with them to attend college full time. He took them up on their offer and moved into their home while he attended school. Similarly, my sister decided she wanted to move in with them as well and made her own plans to attend college. The four of them were living in the home together for several years in Tennessee. My brother attended classes and received his bachelor's degree and later his master's degree. My sister changed her mind and decided not to go the college route, and instead pursued ministry.

I told Brett about my biological father early on in our relationship, and he encouraged me to get a private investigator to seek closure on the issue. He hesitated to believe my mother's story about his involvement in the Mafia simply because he, too, had heard her various tales and noticed something off about the whole scenario.

I had been indoctrinated to feel terrified and scared when I would think of my birth father, so I would abruptly put the kibosh on our conversations without really thinking his proposal through logically.

While I was at work one day, my mother called to tell me that my biological father was on the front page of the *Journal Star*, our local newspaper. Everything got hazy. I started to feel lightheaded and immediately burst into tears.

I left work and met Brett, and the two of us went to my mother's house for further explanation. My heart was racing. I was sobbing hysterically. And simultaneously, I felt relieved that maybe this was finally it: all the answers I'd been seeking.

The man on the front of the page was an infamous Mafia member in Chicago named "Joey the Clown," which did not match the name she'd given me all these years. When we started to question my mother, she quickly shot us down and demanded that we leave her home, immediately.

"I'm done talking now. Get out of my house."

She was curt and refused to discuss the matter any further. I left in a state of shock, further traumatized, and confused about the narrative she'd told me all of these years. Brett, again, offered to find a private investigator, stating, "This isn't right, what she's doing to you."

HEALING, LOVE, AND SCHOOL

But I still came to my mother's defense, like a parrot trapped in a cage, snapping back at him, reciting verbatim her old excuses for mistreating me. "He was an angry, violent man who hurt my mother." I mimicked the dialogue I'd been fed.

I couldn't help but wonder why she called to tell me this, if she was only going to silence me, yet again?

Soon after this encounter, I fell asleep and suddenly, as I had been in the dream with Cuddles, I felt transported to another place. I was standing in the longest line I'd ever seen and was immediately annoyed. The room was completely dark. The only light came from a giant, movie theater-sized screen. I could see another person standing on a platform directly in front of the screen. What I couldn't see as well was a very large being seated and facing the person on the platform. Taking this all in, I tapped the woman in the line in front of me and said, "If they have to go through each of our entire lives on that screen, this is going to take forever." She replied, "Well, we're dead. We have forever."

My stomach sank into my body and the worst feeling I'd ever had in my entire life overtook me. I was shaking and in shock and the only thought I had was, "Oh, no, I didn't accomplish my purpose."

Just as quickly as I could start to process what was happening, suddenly, it was me on the platform and my life on the screen. The very large being suddenly asked, "What have you done for your fellow man?"

His voice sounded like thunder and His words boomed with authority. I knew this was God. Panic set in as I tried to grapple for a response worthy of His question, and I knew I hadn't achieved what I was sent to the Earth to do. Then I woke up.

I knew this was more than just some random dream. I had truly never felt more grateful to be alive and grappled with what it could mean, and

MY FATHER'S FEATHERS

started to think again, about destiny and how I was helping others. I knew God was real, but what did it look like to truly follow Him in our modern society without the confining and rigid religious constraints I saw in the church system? Was I wrong about church? Had I simply not found the right one?

CHAPTER 9

Lincoln and My Grandfather

When Brett and I had been married for a year, we decided to try to have a baby. We only tried for a couple months when I screamed for Brett and he came running, thinking something was wrong. Instead, I started jumping up and down, showing him the positive pregnancy test.

I couldn't help but think of the last time I'd seen a positive pregnancy test, and how very different I felt. So, the moment was bittersweet for me.

When I was around thirteen weeks pregnant, I started bleeding so heavily I had to leave work. We immediately went and got a sonogram, and it confirmed everything looked normal, but I had to be closely monitored going forward. Throughout the remainder of the pregnancy, the bleeding would suddenly start up again. I never knew when it would happen or why it was happening, but it was frequent enough to make me a nervous wreck, worrying that something was wrong with my baby.

I felt like maybe I was being punished for my abortion and maybe I didn't deserve children. My gynecologist could not find an explanation.

One day, I was in the bathroom at home and noticed the bleeding had started again. My heart dropped into my stomach and a rush of panic set in. I started crying and pleaded to the Lord: "Please, God. I can endure the bleeding the rest of the pregnancy if you will just confirm everything will be okay with this baby, and he will get here safely. Please give me peace to handle this pregnancy because I've never been this scared or worried before in my life."

I said "he" because I strongly felt I was having a boy immediately after I got pregnant. I just knew. We were looking at boy names and on the top of the list was Lincoln, which also happened to be a family name on my husband's side. We hadn't officially found out the sex of the baby yet.

When I walked out of the restroom and down the hallway to the living room, I saw Brett seated on the couch watching the nightly news. Playing on the large television was a politician seated and being interviewed, and in the background was the largest hanging picture of President Abraham Lincoln I'd ever seen.

Suddenly, like being struck with a lightening flow of information, I was hit with the facts: We were having a boy, his name would be Lincoln, and he would be healthy.

I started crying with shock and wonder and relayed the news to a very stunned Brett. He looked at me like a deer caught in the headlights, but I said, "I know this to be true like I know my name is MacKenzie, but I can't explain how I know, I just do. God just told me."

I didn't hear a specific voice; it was more like a solidified knowing I didn't have previously. The sonogram also revealed we were having a boy, and I continued to have several bleeding episodes to follow, but I was given such peace that I no longer felt worry or panic accompanying the episodes. I was able to feel excitement despite my condition and looked forward to meeting my son.

I gave birth to a perfectly healthy, ten-pound boy named Lincoln on July 6, 2011.

I was drained following the prolonged, intense labor and birth of my son. Lincoln was my mother's first grandchild, but instead of staying in town and getting to know him, she decided it would be a good time a few days after his birth to visit my siblings in Tennessee.

I was having a hard time recovering, and in my emotional state, I wished more than anything my mother was there to help me and give me advice. I think the culmination of all of the times I had needed and wanted her to be there for me was hitting me all at once in the days immediately following Lincoln's birth. Thankfully, my mother-in-law stayed with us and helped, but it still wasn't the same as having my own mother care for me.

When I looked in the mirror and saw my post-baby body, it shocked me. The days were so dark following the birth of my son. I fell into a dark depression. The darkness stole my ability to function normally, and worse, to breastfeed my son.

As I went to bed one night shortly after his birth, torn open by new wounds inflicted by my mother's absence when I needed her, yet again, the thought that my son would not have the opportunity to meet his biological grandfather crossed my mind for the first time. That reality saddened me and I entered into a new level of grieving at his mysterious whereabouts, and thinking about how I'd explain all of this to Lincoln. It wasn't fair that now my sweet, innocent baby would be deprived.

So many buried emotions surfaced within me on this particular night, with the realization that I would no longer be the only one directly affected by his absence. I cried deep, heaving sobs into my pillow. I was beside myself, tossing the covers on and off uneasily in my bed, trying to come to terms with an impossible situation.

When I finally exhausted myself emotionally, I collapsed into a deep sleep. Just as quickly, as I drifted off to sleep in my own bed, I was again transported somewhere else. I knew I was on the bottom level of a boat, seated, and that I could not move or get up from where I was sitting. I knew all of this information without anyone speaking a word to me. The person seated to my right drank heavily out of a paper bag, to the point of vomiting, then passed out and died. To my horror, I watched as he regained consciousness, woke up, realized where he was, and became devastated on finding his current circumstances unchanged. He started drinking again, to the point of vomiting, then passed out and died.

I could barely catch my breath once I realized that he was trapped here in this vicious cycle of abusing alcohol and couldn't escape.

I also had the understanding there was to be no conversation with anyone on the boat. Shifting my focus from the man with the bottle of alcohol, my eyes darted across the room, taking in more horror. I witnessed others injecting needles in their arms, shaking violently, dying, waking up, and repeating the same process.

I soon understood that everyone on the boat was partying in some way and dying and coming back to life, only to repeat this process again and again. The look of relief on their faces right before they died was replaced immediately with the grief and sheer terror of the depths of agony when it hit them that they were back to life again. Each time they were about to die, they were filled with hope that this endless cycle would end, only to have their hopes crushed and dashed by coming back to life again just long enough to overdose.

The realization that I had no escape started to settle over me, and just as it did, I looked over to my left and that's when I saw him.

Shining and emitting bright, rainbow-tinted light was Paul's dad, my grandfather, who was a pastor during his time on Earth. He had died the previous year, in 2010, and I was not particularly close to him, even though he never missed a single basketball game during my career. I always assumed he didn't love me as much as all of his other grandchildren, based on what my mother told me because I was not his biological granddaughter.

Light burst forth from him in every direction and he lit up the entire room with his presence. His smile was huge, and he was young and full of vitality, but it was like an ageless youth, where he simultaneously looked exactly like I remembered him. He was not only full of love: He was LOVE.

I threw my arms around him, relieved that I could move for the first time since I had been on the boat. Something about his presence was releasing me from the confines I had known: No talking and no moving up until this point in this place.

He said with a giggle while his gaze panned the room, "Wow, you have some crazy dreams!"

He laughed with a carefree, effortless tone that soothed me and my worries immediately. I started crying and apologizing for so many things because I saw how clearly wrong I had been about him during our time spent together on Earth. I could feel the truth of how much he loved me right then and there on the boat, and I had never felt anything like it.

I sobbed about how I behaved at his funeral, showing up after a few drinks and numb to his death, and felt such regret to have missed out on this amazing man who clearly loved me so very much. I blubbered on for a very long time.

All the while he just looked at me lovingly. Then he smiled and said, "**All that matters is love**, MacKenzie. Now let's get you off this boat."

He took me by the hand. I got up and we walked to the upper level. I observed it was nighttime, the boat was parked and tied to a dock, and there was a black stretch limousine waiting for me. He led me to the limo, I got in, and woke up.

Immediately, I wanted to go back. I knew I had seen my grandfather, and I had so many more questions to ask him. The love I felt blew me away. I knew I had experienced a supernatural love and worried that since my grandpa was dead, I'd never be able to feel that loved again. I grieved a love I thought was out of my reach and beyond the grave. Little did I know this was only the beginning of his appearances to me in dreams.

After that night, I felt a shift and a restored hope inside me I couldn't explain. The darkness I had struggled with after my son's birth no longer seemed to plague me and render me as incapacitated as it had before. Within a month, I was back on my feet and resumed working full-time.

CHAPTER 10

My Brother's Wedding

In January 2012, I had landed a new full-time sales position with a Fortune 500 company. The office was completely done in glass and the desks were ergonomically correct, meaning you could sit or stand at them, all with the touch of a button. I had a lot of hope for my new role and position in new-accounts development.

By the third week, I was starting to understand my role involved basically cold calling on different accounts and asking if they'd be interested in switching transportation providers. I got hung up on all day long, every day. Rejection was my new role in the office, and I spent time here and there crying in the bathroom. But I didn't stop pursuing new leads. I'd manage to pull myself back together, return to the business floor, and continue to call, day after day.

As time went on, I had acquired a couple new accounts for my company and gained a bit of confidence in my abilities in sales. I liked sales but didn't see a lot of opportunity for upward mobility in my current role. I started looking for new opportunities, and by July of 2012, I accepted another full-time role in donor recruitment with the American Red Cross.

In September 2012, my brother got married in Tennessee. I was elated when my sister-in-law asked me to be a member of the bridal party because up to that point, I had struggled to connect with her.

Living in Illinois provided a logistical challenge for sure, but in addition to that, I sensed there was another reason.

During this time, my dad, my stepmom, sister, and brother were all living under the same roof. Before meeting my brother's girlfriend, I had learned secondhand information about her from my sister, who met Belle first.

"She's kind of quiet and reserved," my sister said, while shrugging her shoulders. "You know, she's sweet, but she's ... not like us. She really lacks self-confidence and struggles with insecurity so don't think it's you if she avoids you or struggles to maintain eye contact. That's just how she is. I've been working with her to try and get her confidence up and be more assertive."

When she talked about Belle, my sister spoke with a tone implying she pitied and felt sorry for her in some way. Belle was more like a wounded little lamb that she was tending to, and a pet project she had generously decided to take on and mentor. I struggled to grasp the actual reality of the situation, having not met her and living in another state entirely. I knew from my own experience with my sister that there was probably more to this story.

Regardless, I did my best to remain optimistic about Belle, and hoped to form a sisterhood bond with her I was never able to attain with my own sister. I longed for a relationship with a sister that was not something painful to be endured, but something that could bring abundance, positivity, and the ability to create memories together that we could look back on with fondness, instead of bringing to mind recollections of more pain and harsh words.

The first thing that struck me when I met Belle was her beauty. Standing tall around 5'10", she was stunning, slender, elegant, and clearly smitten with my brother. It was easy to see why my brother was so in love with her. He absolutely beamed when he looked at her and he laughed effortlessly around her. He gently spoke to her and sweetly gushed about how they had met; the excitement he had for his newfound relationship with her was evident.

Although her words were kind in our conversation, I felt like I was picking up on something else, and noted she struggled to maintain eye contact with me as she spoke. Thinking back to my sister's words, I reminded myself that "she's just shy and insecure."

I brushed off that "something else" I felt during our initial meeting and was soon elated to hear that Owen had proposed to Belle. They decided to get married at my dad and stepmom's home in Tennessee, a sprawling estate with acres of land with beautifully manicured landscaping, something my dad maintained and took care of by himself, by hand.

After a nine-and-a-half-hour drive to Tennessee, Brett and I arrived at my father's house on the day of the rehearsal dinner. I had to use the restroom, so I got out of the vehicle, quickly greeted everyone, and went inside.

"WHERE ARE YOU GOING?"

A man I didn't know chased me down as I entered my father's house. His tone demanded an explanation. Taken aback, I replied, "I have to use the restroom."

He argued with me and continued, "Well, there's no time for that. You have to come outside now. We are getting started."

My sister followed swiftly behind him, echoing, "Come on MacKenzie, get outside. You can hold it."

I continued onward in my quest for the restroom regardless. She continued to yell, beg, and plead with me outside the door. As I emerged successful from the restroom and joined the wedding party on the lawn, I was met with hostile expressions.

"What did I do to these people?" I thought to myself.

To my surprise, I found out the man that chased me to the restroom was the pastor officiating my brother's wedding. This experience served to further confirm my skepticism about the church system.

The following day, I headed next door, where Belle was getting ready, to thank her for including me in the big day. A woman I had never met was standing guard.

"Who are you?" she asked.

I replied, "Owen's sister."

She contorted her face and said with a snarl and an eye roll, "Ugh, you're the half-sister."

"Excuse me?" I replied in disbelief, the breath knocked out of me. "Is Belle here?"

She replied dismissively, "She is, but you can't see her."

I turned around and walked away, mortified and in pieces.

I ran upstairs and grabbed Brett to tell him what had just happened, in complete disbelief.

"Who is running around down here telling everyone I'm their 'half-sister?' I was raised just the same as them in the same family from day one, and these people are treating me like I'm not even in my own family. I don't even know what to say. I'm in such shock."

Suddenly the pastor's inappropriate behavior was starting to make more sense. Most people to my knowledge who knew our family had no idea we weren't full siblings because it was something no one discussed, at least not with me. Why was this a discussion being had behind my back, in another state, with people I didn't know when no one would discuss it with me? I felt sick as I struggled to made it through dinner and quickly found my father by the pool, after many had dispersed.

I told him what had happened, and immediately he became angry over the injustice I had suffered. He reassured me, "You have always been my daughter. From the first moment I saw you, you were my daughter. I love you, MacKenzie, and have never thought of you as any less."

His words were like ointment on the wound that had been ripped open only hours earlier. I felt so grateful to have him right then, as night fell with us sitting outside talking. My dad called over my sister to question her and she immediately denied any implication about her involvement. When she walked away, my sister's best friend at the time admitted Ivy was the one who had told her about my paternity, so I knew she was lying.

Is that what she'd been doing down here for these past few years? Narrating the biography of my life by casting me as the villainous half-sister? I knew, biologically, that she was my half-sibling, but we never openly referred to each other with that label.

Later, she looked me square in the eyes and said "MacKenzie, I would NEVER say anything about that to anyone. I know how much it hurts you and I would NEVER do that."

It felt worse when she was able to lie straight to my face, and that scared me for her. I lost a lot of hope for my relationship with my sister right in that moment, right as she felt she could lie to my face about something that cut me so deep, about something, by her own admission, she knew hurt me more than anything. To my knowledge, no one besides my father spoke to my sister about this afterward. This was simply one more time she continued to bully me with my own biology.

I was deeply wounded at the insinuation a stranger made that I was a shameful part of my own family. True, I had a different biological father, but Paul's name was on my birth certificate and he was there the day I was born and has been there ever since.

I was shaken to the core and felt exposed and unsafe. My biology ruined everything for me, continuously. Now, it had hunted me down and followed me all the way to another state. I couldn't get away from it and the questions that lurked remained unanswered and unprocessed.

MY FATHER'S FEATHERS

The old feelings pertaining to my biological father were welling up within me, sparked by the altercation with a stranger. I felt deeply betrayed and humiliated on a new, low level, but I had to put on my blue bridesmaid dress and my best smiling face to get ready for the wedding.

Standing out in the hot Tennessee heat, I listened to the man who had chased me to the restroom officiate my brother's wedding. I looked over at my sister's smiling face, and the events from the day before reverberated in my mind, cycling, swishing, circling, taunting me. I did my best to shift my attention to my brother and focus on the events of the wedding, but the fact that I felt like, overall, in our relationship to date, he could care less about me welled up inside, so that wasn't working, either.

I was being consumed by the pain of it all, like a disease overtaking my body. The internal dialogue playing during the ceremony was overwhelming me, and I began to feel lightheaded as I stood.

"This is not happening; this is not happening..."

Panic overtook me and, to my total horror, I almost passed out. I clumsily balanced myself on the edge of a cement portion of one of the tall pillars closest to me to keep from falling. I felt humiliated.

The next day, we left my father's house. I was in pieces and felt ripped to shreds over my brother's wedding. It was clear to me that my sister had misinformed several people about her notion of who I was before my arrival. Their behavior and treatment towards me were starting to make more sense, now.

I called my mother in the car while I was distraught and she simply recited her catch-all phrase in regards to our relationship in response: "I just wish you girls would get along."

At this point, it was simply a reflex for my mother to blame me, too, when my sister behaved poorly. I felt further misunderstood and unloved by my mother's response.

When I hung up, I stared at my husband behind the wheel as he drove us home. Appreciation welled up in my soul as I recognized that I was no longer alone when these situations occurred. My husband was there, listening and comforting me the best that he could the entire way home. He always tried his best to understand and speak gently and offer his support. I realized I had finally found someone who would be there for me and someone who saw the abuse I was continually enduring at the hands of my family members. It wasn't all in my head and I was not crazy, over-emotional, or irrational – all labels that had been placed on me to excuse my family's mistreatment. Brett's partnership meant newfound freedom from a burden I had carried silently by myself for years.

CHAPTER 11

Sins of the Father

I couldn't wait to see Keanu Reeve's new movie, *John Wick*. I extended an invite to my sister to come watch it when it came out in theaters in 2014, then have lunch. Ever since the release of *The Matrix*, I watched and waited to see what projects Keanu was involved with because I viewed him as a fellow seeker. I felt like there was more than meets the eye with projects he took on and in films and the roles he played, so I was eager to check out his latest choice.

My sister accepted the invite, and I went and saw Keanu again in action. I enjoyed *John Wick* immensely because he was determined and unstoppable in his quest to pursue justice. He kept fighting no matter how the odds seemed to be stacked continually against him. He refused to back down and he never quit.

Ivy leaned over and commented to me in disgust as I excitedly watched the movie: "You just love violence, don't you?"

She didn't get it. It wasn't the fighting that propelled me to want to watch this movie; it was because of Keanu Reeves and the film choice he had selected that got me curious to watch *John Wick*. I liked seeking buried nuggets of wisdom and insight in his movies.

We left the theatre and went and had lunch at the Olive Garden where she proceeded to ream me for my film selection. "You have angry blood, you know," she casually said between bites of food.

"Excuse me?" I tried to keep calm, despite feeling hurt.

"Sins of the father; you've heard about that, right? Your biological father was angry, and so are you. And it's why you like violent movies."

She caught me off-guard. I was looking to bond and get closer with someone who clearly had a lot of issues with me.

I knew this, but my desperate desire to be close with her and have a good relationship always left me feeling blindsided. It felt like I was trying to climb a brutally high mountain relentlessly and with great effort, but I could never make it to the top because I was constantly thwarted regardless of my determination.

"I feel like you are painting me into a corner," I responded. "I don't know how it wouldn't anger anyone to be accused of having 'angry blood.' If I told you this conversation didn't make me angry, then I'd be lying."

I restrained myself with great effort from giving her a real piece of my mind.

In 2014, I was still working full-time at the American Red Cross in a position that I absolutely loved most days. I had my own territory consisting of several counties and traveled and spoke to high schools and grade schools about the importance of donating blood. I worked with teams of volunteers to coordinate the blood drives and recruited donors by several different methods. I felt like I had a purpose and was helping others to achieve a greater good. I was a part of a team, and my manager made me feel welcome and encouraged me in my new role.

Her trust in my capabilities in my position helped me to believe I was an important member of a team, once again. I was elated to get a piece of me back that I felt I had lost once my basketball days ended.

On the home front, now three, Lincoln brought me great joy. I was completely undone by my son's pure, innocent heart and zest for life. I was seeing the world differently through his eyes and enjoying watching him learn and explore.

However, I'd neglected my body and overall care of myself while my marriage, son, and full-time job didn't seem to leave much time for maintenance of any kind and was struggling to lose the seventy-five pounds of extra weight I'd put on since pregnancy.

At my height, I could carry a little more weight than an average-sized woman, but at three hundred pounds, I was past those limits. I was experiencing joint pain in my knees and struggling to make it up and down our stairs at home without breathing heavily. I tried diet plan after diet plan. Nothing seemed to work and I found myself hungrier and weighing more than I did before starting each time. I was addicted to fast food and sugar and did not seem to possess the capability to tear myself away. When I made brownies, I ate the whole pan. I kept buying bigger and bigger clothing sizes.

Brett and I decided to stop at one child, but Lincoln regularly requested a sister at every given opportunity. We decided to start trying for another baby, driven by our son's insistence about a sister. He never asked for a brother; always a sister and always with such certainty. I explained to my sweet boy that we could not guarantee a girl, but he was certain that was exactly what I would have next.

Simultaneously, Lincoln would often speak about God, seemingly out of nowhere; we were not involved in church at this time. I did speak about God in our home from time to time, but Lincoln talked about heaven like he knew it and he spoke about God as if He were in the room with us. He spoke so eloquently and his insights were so simple, beautiful, and refreshing that I wanted to know God more intimately, like my son clearly knew Him.

Brett was raised with a Catholic upbringing, so he, too, was a believer and was open to pursuing some local churches in the area to see if any were a good fit. We made the rounds and toured and attended several area churches, but none felt quite right for our family.

After a year of trying to get pregnant with no success, I went to the gynecologist and had a procedure to check my ovaries. They deemed everything was functioning properly and put me on a fertility drug called Clomid. There was no diagnosed reason they could see as to why I wasn't able to get pregnant again. Still, month after month, the pregnancy tests showed negative.

We became co-owners of a Buffalo Wild Wings restaurant (where we originally met), so I was excited to leave my full-time job at the Red Cross and stay home with Lincoln. Freed from the time constraints of a full-time work schedule for the first time since being a mother, and at thirty-four-years old, I knew I had to do something to get in better shape – and see if my poor nutrition and lack of exercise could possibly be playing a contributing role in preventing me from getting pregnant.

Motivated to pursue fitness in an effort to get pregnant, I'd pick Lincoln up from preschool around 10:00 a.m. and we'd head to the gym, which had a daycare facility. I'd run on the treadmill for an hour and we'd be on our way. I had also started a new nutrition program and did this every day during the week for a few months.

We also prayed to God that we would be able to conceive another child and were starting to look at our options in terms of adoption.

At first, taking the pregnancy test was something I enjoyed. Then, after the fourth month of receiving a negative test, I started to dread it – and, again, I started to wonder if it was because I had an abortion that I would not be able to have further children. The guilt started to set in and the pregnancy tests became sheer torment from that point on.

It was all I could do to keep from full-on sobbing as the seconds ticked by, painfully slow, while I waited for the results to appear in the window on the test. I'd sometimes take another two or three to make sure that they were really negative, hoping maybe that one had been wrong.

SINS OF THE FATHER

On Good Friday in 2016, the Lord answered our prayers again.

The pain and agony I'd experienced in waiting the past year-and-a-half were all gone in an instant with news of a positive test. **To my surprise, the waiting and the pain had birthed more joy** through finding out now I was pregnant.

We worked hard and saved for ten years to buy our dream home, and now with a second baby on the way, the timing was perfect. We decided on a new home with all the bells and whistles in an amazing school district, still in our hometown of Peoria, Ill. It came complete with an iron-rod fence for our mini goldendoodle, Willie Nelson.

Suddenly, the dream life I had envisioned seemed like it was falling into place. Now, we were practically across the street from one of the biggest churches locally; it sits on nearly sixty acres of land. According to their description on the website: "The grounds feature a variety of park-like features available for nearby neighbors, including a playground, walking path, disc golf course and basketball and sand volleyball courts."

Simultaneously, I had reconnected with an old friend from high school, Regina, who happened to attend the church. Her enthusiasm persuaded me to give the church a second look, and we started to regularly attend services.

I tried to stay active during my pregnancy and to keep running and walking, but I had an episode of very heavy bleeding about ten weeks in, and I was terrified I'd lost her.

"I don't think I can handle another pregnancy like this; please Lord, not again."

I prayed desperately. Thankfully, the Lord spared me and I didn't miscarry, but the singular episode made me nervous moving forward to do anything strenuous that might jeopardize the pregnancy, and my gynecologist agreed.

But "taking it easy" meant I picked back up the sugar, the sweets, and the indulgences I used to love so much before I lost some weight. As the remainder of my pregnancy went on, I continued to gain weight. In addition, I got severely ill and had a hard time breathing due to the heavy cough I'd developed, and had to use an inhaler regularly to get relief.

Little did I know, this was only the precursor for many more health problems on the horizon.

CHAPTER 12

Medical Challenges and Nevada

Throughout my pregnancy, everywhere I went, whether it was picking up Lincoln from school, shopping, or socializing, I would hear the name Chloe. I realized it was a somewhat common name, but it sounded like it was being highlighted to me because it was louder, clearer, crisper, and more pronounced than the other words.

A feeling swept over me like a warm, welcoming, gentle breeze when I heard her name. I felt a familiarity and an understanding that somehow, she was a part of me. It was happening so frequently that I finally decided to pray and ask God.

"Is Chloe to be this baby girl's name?"

In response, I heard, "No, she is up in heaven with me."

And I knew. I cried and I knew exactly who Chloe was.

At the time, my smart boy was fascinated with geography. Lincoln suggested Nevada as a name for his sister, and after I looked up the Spanish meaning, I discovered it meant "covered in snow." My due date was coincidentally in December. When I went into labor and was almost ready to deliver her, a nurse announced in quiet awe, knowing the name we'd picked and its meaning: "It's just started snowing."

When Nevada came out to greet the world and make her grand appearance, the same nurse noted, "The snow just stopped."

Peace washed over me at the meaning of her name and the coinciding snow that fell and stopped during the duration of her birth. It was confirmation to me that Lincoln had picked the perfect name for his sister.

To date, she is a joyful, vibrant five-year-old who prefers to be called "Vada" and loves snow more than anyone I know.

After her birth, I desperately wanted to breastfeed Vada because I didn't get the opportunity with Lincoln due to battling postpartum depression. When we brought her home and I attempted to feed her, the pain in my stomach was unbelievably acute. I cried and fought back painful tears the whole time, and didn't understand why it was so unbearable. We bought formula and I felt like a failure, yet again, for being unable to breastfeed another one of my babies.

After a week of persistent suffering, I went back to my gynecologist's office, but she wasn't available, so I saw a nurse on staff who I'd not met previously.

"I'm having so much pain in my abdomen and I have a fever daily. I'm really struggling," I said, very concerned.

She replied flatly, "Well, you've just had a baby, and it will be painful."

"I know, she's my second baby..."

I trailed off despondently. I felt so disconnected from my own reality and did not feel like myself. I was barely eating.

"I'll prescribe you some antibiotics and that should fix you up," she said resolutely. I felt there was no getting past it, and I was in so much pain, I didn't really want to be examined at this point anyway. I reluctantly took the prescription, feeling too poorly to argue, and left her office.

A few days later, I was still struggling and the pain was worse. I felt more and more out of it all the time, and all I wanted to do was sleep. I looked pale and I had big circles under my eyes. Food tasted foreign and bland and I spent a lot of time thinking about why everything had suddenly turned to cardboard, not realizing my body was shutting down. I was bleeding so much that I struggled to keep up with the sanitary pad changes.

Christmas was approaching, and I talked to my mother on the phone about the gathering she was having at her house.

"Mom, I may not be able to make Christmas. I'm really not feeling well," I shared with her.

"What?! You have to be here. That's not an option, MacKenzie. Your brother and his family are traveling a long way to be here with all of us. You have to come!"

I knew if I didn't show up on Christmas, she would make me pay the price for my disobedience. When I got off the phone with her, I cried because I wondered if this is what dying felt like, and because I saw where her concern lied: making sure she had a perfect Christmas family gathering, and not with my well-being. I cried because I felt so terrible. I could not even think rationally about the situation anyway. So, I went back to sleep.

Christmas morning came, and I was barely able to get out of bed. Driven by fear of my mother's disapproval, I mustered every ounce of my strength to get ready to go to her house. I asked my in-laws to come watch Nevada because I couldn't even bend over without being subjected to excruciating pain, so she did not attend.

My mother is a fantastic cook and always has been, but her Christmas lunch tasted like sandpaper – similar to everything I had attempted to eat for the past week-and-a-half. Sitting upright at her table, I could feel myself drifting in and out of consciousness. I struggled to engage fully in conversation with other family.

As we moved to a sitting room to unwrap our presents, I leaned my head on Brett's shoulder and tried my best not to fall asleep. Every movement hurt, but I smiled for pictures, cramming the pain down, biting my lip to avoid grimacing, and trying my best to ignore the "You're dying! You're dying!" alarms my body was sounding.

I could feel I was fighting a losing battle at that point, and I was in big trouble. Regardless, I summoned every ounce of remaining energy I had to act invested and interested in the holiday festivities.

My mother refuses to acknowledge everyone's uniqueness, to the point where she buys the same gifts for my sister and me every year. She's been doing this since I was a little kid. Regardless of what I asked for, she would constantly buy me and my sister the same items, with little regard for specific requests.

Ivy, Belle, my stepsister, and I proceeded to awkwardly unwrap one matching lingerie piece after another. Finally, we went home, where I crawled back into my bed, on the first Christmas with our new baby.

I barely got any sleep that night because the pain was so intense. Brett took me to the ER the next day. It was packed to the point where there was nowhere to sit down, but I knew I was in such poor condition I couldn't possibly stand until someone could see me. A worker took pity on me, got me a stretcher, and left me in the hallway.

Finally, they wheeled me into my own room, and the ER doctor came over to inspect me.

"What seems to be the problem?"

I described my symptoms and he replied in the same manner the nurse had a week ago: "Well, yes, ma'am, you've just had a baby, it's going to be painful for a while. I'll get you some antibiotics and you can be on your way."

I KNEW something was very wrong and my body was starting to shut down. This time, I stood my ground and advocated for myself.

"No!" I exclaimed. "I'm not leaving without an examination. Something is very wrong."

He looked offended by my insistence, but knew I wasn't leaving without a fight. I knew the ER was busy, but if I left without an exam, I feared I might not be alive to come back another time.

MEDICAL CHALLENGES AND NEVADA

"Okay," he sighed, and reluctantly agreed, rolling his eyes.

He grabbed the spectrum and inserted it. I screamed in agony.

"I ... I ... I am so sorry..." he trailed off.

He immediately turned to his assistant and whispered something to her, and they quickly transported me to a sonogram room. I took a minute to take in the moment and tearfully told Brett, "No day could ever possibly be as bad as this day. Remind me to think on this anytime I am complaining about anything, ever, and it will pale in comparison to this."

The sonogram showed some placenta had been left behind and was now infecting my uterus. I was placed in my own room, and since it was on the infectious disease floor, I was not allowed to be with my newborn baby. I pleaded with them to put me on a floor where I could be with her, but the hospital staff said that wasn't possible.

Alone in my room with my husband at home caring for our children, I thought a lot about my life up to this point and how quickly it almost ended. What if I hadn't stood up to the doctor in the ER and gone home instead? What had it all been for? The profound shock about how short life truly is hit me in that moment in my hospital room.

Suddenly, I had a new perspective on life and death, and I vowed I would never forget how close I came to not being here anymore. I thought of Chloe, and how I felt there was something I had to do for her, still, on this Earth, but what was I being called to do for her?

I prayed to the Lord to guide me and help me achieve my purpose and destiny on this Earth.

The next day, I underwent a dilation and curettage procedure to get the remainder of the placenta removed. In addition, the surgeon noted the stitches I had received after I gave birth to Nevada were not properly done, so she removed them and stitched me up again.

The day after the procedure, I was finally reunited with my newborn baby girl. I thought about my mother's lack of concern following my hospitalization and the jolting, stunning reality of the magnitude of her callousness hit me harder than the extreme fatigue I was feeling trying to recover at home.

Making matters worse, sounds, lights, and especially my sweet daughter's cries were magnified and interpreted as overwhelming now by my body. I hoped with some time, I'd be back to feeling like I did before my pregnancy with Vada.

I still had another remaining, lingering issue that needed to be dealt with from my pregnancy. An abscess of sorts, which was later deemed a "pregnancy tumor," had formed on my tongue. The day of the procedure, the doctor numbed my tongue, then came at me with scissors in hand. It took a few attempts before I stopped using my legs, arms, hands, and everything else to push him off of me. I could feel the tugging and pulling as he cut into my tongue and removed the abscess. It was a brutal procedure that left me with stitches and nightmares.

It hurt immensely in the days that followed, and I struggled to be at home with my baby all day and to try and keep up with my son who was now five, while simultaneously keeping our home clean, doing laundry, cooking, and performing other normal household duties. Brett worked full-time at the restaurant we co-owned. I constantly had a pounding, pulsating headache, felt like I hadn't slept in years, and my body ached in an unfamiliar way I hadn't experienced prior to my pregnancy.

"What is happening to me?" I'd wonder, feeling trapped inside my own body and useless as a wife and mother. I felt like I was trapped in my own hellish version of Groundhog Day and there was no escape. Shouldn't I be recovered by now? Would I recover?

I would call my husband at work and cry and beg and plead for him to come home and help me. I knew I couldn't continue in my current condition to care for my newborn daily. I saw the writing on the wall: We had to put her in daycare, at least part-time.

I felt like a failure in every sense of the word. I was excited to capitalize on the opportunity to stay home and snuggle my sweet baby girl, but I couldn't even enjoy doing that, now.

Adding insult to injury, I felt further humiliated communicating the news to family and friends. But I did my best to put a positive spin on the news. The truth was, I was physically unwell and struggling to understand the underlying cause of this persistent, chronic pain that I was wracked with in every moment. I felt overridden by guilt that no matter how hard I tried to fight through my fatigue and pain, it was still dominating my life.

Four months after Vada was born, in April of 2017, I decided to take the drastic action of committing myself to an evening, ten-week kickboxing course. I wanted to be with my daughter every day and feel well enough to enjoy our time together, so I was willing to do whatever it took to push past my physical symptoms.

Some days, I would sleep an entire day while Nevada was at daycare in order to get the strength to work out, but I completed the course and even continued my fitness journey with kickboxing after the course was over. In addition, I was working out with a trainer taking CrossFit courses, but I continued to struggle physically regardless.

The dream home and life I had envisioned felt more like a prison. I was battling with every ounce of strength to make it through one more day with crippling fatigue and pain, specifically in my jaw, neck, shoulders, and back.

I went to an ENT specialist locally who diagnosed me with TMJ and referred me to a jaw specialist. As a new patient, they took a scan of my mouth and sinus area to fit me with a specialized mouthpiece that was supposed to help my pain. When the CT scan results came back, the doctor told me that it showed a concerning mass in my sinus cavity and he recommended I get further testing done.

I was devastated leaving my appointment, wondering what this could mean. After exploring Google for further information, I was terrified.

CHAPTER 13

Tell Mom, "She is Going to be Okay."

I was so shaken by this news. It was all I could think about as I met my son in our front yard as he got off of the bus from kindergarten. On that same October day in 2017, I sat down with Lincoln at our kitchen table to chat with him while he ate his snack.

Before I could ask him any questions about his day, he looked at me very seriously and shared, "Hey Mom, I was at school today and we were sitting on the reading rug listening to our teacher tell us a Halloween story. All of the sudden, I heard this voice as loud as a whisper say, "Tell Mom she is going to be okay.'"

I sat in silence and simply took in the moment with Lincoln, somehow knowing this was a huge moment, one that was going to change many things for me moving forward.

Lincoln clearly said he specifically heard the voice say, "Tell Mom," not, "Mom will be okay." My sweet boy was on a mission to deliver a message sitting at the kitchen table that day. I had my own experiences in the past knowing things I knew there was no possible way I could have known, but hearing my son talk about a voice being as loud as a whisper hit me differently.

Was God really speaking directly to my little boy about me? I marveled over this, and decided yes, he had heard from the Lord. He told me over and over so matter-of-factly, and I could tell he was somewhat confused by my astonishment of him relaying this message.

Lincoln had no way of knowing about my appointment earlier on the same day, or the disturbing news I had received in regards to my sinus mass. I clung to God's reassurance delivered through my son like the truth I knew it to be in my soul, and would go back to this day in my mind many, many times for needed encouragement.

"You're going to be okay, MacKenzie, you are," I'd say to myself. "Just keep going, just keep moving."

But there were days I'd absolutely crumple into a ball on the floor, a mess of tears, snot, and wails, and I didn't know how I was going to come out of that place. I didn't know if this was the day where I couldn't survive to see the next, and I was terrified in those moments.

When the nurse called with more news of my sinus tumor, she said, "You will be okay," further confirming what I felt like God was speaking to Lincoln over me.

The news cut both ways: The mass was not causing any issues, but I was still in a great deal of physical pain with no solid underlying cause.

During a CrossFit training session, I threw my back out. It was a severe strain and required crutches to walk, muscle relaxers for the spasming pain, doctor visits, and physical therapy. Every time I went to sit, stand, or lie down, my back took the opportunity to remind me that it was working against me. Somedays even breathing hurt.

I was sent into a place of deep depression that no matter how hard I was trying and fighting for my life and physical well-being, I felt constantly sabotaged by pain and circumstances out of my control. I no longer had the ability to keep working out physically, so yet another lifeline and avenue I was pursuing at this time was taken. I was worse off physically and more hurt at this point than before I started to work out.

I was told by the jaw specialist to give the appliance time to work. I kept wearing it at their insistence, still believing this was going to solve my problems, although the truth was I was feeling even worse wearing the appliance (which we had just paid for out of pocket, since our insurance didn't cover it).

I kept asking them for more help or if there was something else, and when it got really bad, they'd use a large TENS device. They would put me in a leather massage chair, put two pads on the joints of my jaw and one on my neck, and zap me in an attempt to lessen the pain.

I didn't really feel a difference after those sessions and started to feel so frustrated as my pain with the appliance increased more and more. All the while, they assured me this was part of the process and to just keep letting it do its work.

Simultaneously, in the fall of 2017, I had made the decision to become more involved at my church by signing up for a women's group, which met on every other Tuesday morning, called The Well. It was also my friend Regina's suggestion. I was exhausted, confused, in pain, and desperate for a lifeline and to find answers to the questions burning in my soul. I craved a deeper understanding of who God was, how He communicated, and to know how He wanted me to walk out my faith. Maybe being surrounded by a group of women seeking answers to these questions that burned in my soul would help?

Even being a huge church skeptic, I was desperate for relief and I felt like it couldn't hurt at this point. I was willing to try anything and I needed to get well for my family.

There were approximately one hundred and fifty women (maybe more or less, I don't know the official numbers) broken up into groups of ten to fifteen, with designated women to lead each table. Regina happened to be a table leader, and I requested to sit at her table since we were already friends.

At first glance and on paper, it seemed The Well was going to be a great match for me and my faith journey. I happened to already know another woman at my table, and my aunt also led another table at the same women's group.

As time went on, I noticed The Well had the same women in leadership speaking consistently. I began to pick up on a culture of these women grouping together, and the more I attended, the more I noticed the praise that was being offered to one another amidst this particular group of women in leadership. Each time a woman would go to speak, she'd make it a point to speak highly of her friend "so and so" and how long they'd known each other, and all about this specific friend.

While it was great that they were such good friends, and I was genuinely happy for them, over time, it became distracting for me. The consistent level to which each woman seemed so invested in giving the next woman credit for where she was at "on the stage" or "look at me now" speaking to everyone … was this the goal we were each to aspire to?

What The Well ended up provoking in me was deep thought about human worship and the role it was playing in the church functions. Was Jesus the focal point at The Well, or was it the women in leadership who led The Well and their friendships with one another?

Besides interacting with Regina at The Well, I was still meeting her for coffees on days that we had some free time. If I wasn't feeling well on the particular day we had scheduled to meet up, I would force myself to get out of the house for some interaction.

She was aware of how I was struggling and happened to sell essential oils. She suggested several natural remedies that could help to promote my healing, and I started to purchase what she suggested. I didn't notice any significant health improvements from using the oils, but I did like how they smelled in the diffuser at my home and continued to purchase lotions, soaps, and toxin-free household products that Regina recommended through the multilevel marketing company she represented. Maybe, as she told me, the toxic products I had in my home were contributing to my pain after all.

I felt like I was helping my friend to make money, and it made me feel good at first to support her in her endeavors as well. I thanked her constantly for her knowledge and recommendations.

I also attended Sunday morning services with my family at church. My pastor at the time, Cal Rychener, spoke a sermon on November 26, 2017, titled "Christmas is Forgiving: Unlocking the Prison." The message was about "When we don't forgive, we make our hearts into a prison. We bind ourselves to our wounds, increase our pain, and invite torment – and we lock the door to God's healing power. Forgiveness unlocks the door, expels the torment, and ushers in the peace and joy of God's renewing grace."

I took a minute when I returned from church that morning and asked God if I was holding anyone hostage in my prison of unforgiveness. To my surprise, an image of my biological father appeared. He was in a jail cell, standing behind iron bars, with his hands on the bars. He had a sad expression on his face, and I knew he'd been kept there for a very long time. I was in total shock that I had never thought to forgive him for abandoning me, and immediately walked over to the jail cell, unlocked the door, and set him free. He had a huge smile on his face and he gave me the biggest hug. It was such a beautiful moment. I watched as he walked past me, and out into the beautiful day that was waiting for him in the sunshine. He turned and looked back at me one last time and was free.

For three days following this forgiveness, I couldn't stop crying, but they weren't sad tears. I felt somehow like I was being healed in the deepest places. Wounds that had been open were starting to close.

The spiritual shift I experienced as a result of forgiving my biological father gave me renewed strength and hope for my physical weight loss and health battle. Forgiving my biological father had set me free too. I found freedom from the prison of my unhealthy eating cycle, and it was much easier to start cooking healthier meals. I wasn't perfect, but had stopped the binge-eating. I felt freshly determined to get the weight off, yet again, only this time, it was only going to happen with what I was eating since working out was still much too painful, with my back still in poor condition.

I didn't starve myself and focused on eating more vegetables, lean protein, and protein shakes. Within a couple months, the numbers on the scale were moving in a positive direction, and I felt empowered to continue in my weight-loss journey with a fresh approach towards healthy eating. It's been a journey towards finding the right workout that I can maintain consistently for me considering my back issues, but I never gave up, regardless of the countless hurdles I faced. I no longer struggle with binge-eating and haven't since the day I forgave my biological father. During the past five years, I've tenaciously fought through various trials and pain, but I've managed to maintain a seventy-five-pound weight loss with no extra measures taken except consistent diet and exercise.

CHAPTER 14

Chronic Pain

I further took Regina's advice and started visiting a chiropractor in hopes that my back would benefit and I could start working out again. I was running from appointment to appointment to try to keep on top of my health and I felt overwhelmed, but managed to consistently manage my eating regardless. For the most part at this point in my chronic-pain journey, I felt my friends and family were trying to be supportive, but as time progressed, the appointments started to stack up and eyebrows began to raise.

I would call my mother when the pain felt so bad, I didn't think I would be able to handle it a minute more. Each time I would reach out begging for help, she'd be shocked and astounded and say things like, "Oh, you're still in pain?" And I'd feel like I was informing her about my condition for the first time all over again.

When I got off the phone with her, the pain was always much more intense than before I called her in the first place. I wish I would have caught on sooner to the fact that feeling worse degrees of pain in my body was being triggered by interactions with my mother.

I felt like I wasn't allowed to talk to her about anything other than what she wanted to discuss. If I brought up a matter she was simply not interested in, or did not care to talk about, she'd shift the focus to something else and stare back at me with a very large smile. I understood what this meant and didn't dare to switch the subject back to the conversation I needed or wanted to have. I'd take a big gulp, fidget with my hands, look at my feet in submission, and do my best to shift gears to contribute to the conversation she desired.

I see now, looking back, how very little she actually knew me, all because she simply wasn't interested in anything but her own needs, wants, and interests.

My mother only listened to tell me what to do and how to proceed, and then it was case closed. I felt pressured to do what she told me to do regardless of how I felt. I knew if I did something to the contrary, she would chastise me the next time I brought up a certain situation. I wasn't looking for her to solve my problem and did not need anyone to decide for me as a fully functioning, successful, adult person with a family. I was looking to spend time and exchange some laughs with her, but we were constantly in a state of conflict because we desired different things. She wanted to assert control and domination. I wanted to share my life and be loved by my mother.

My family was complete, but the life I had worked and tried so hard to maintain and curate was falling apart in front of my very eyes due to my failing health, without any concrete medical explanation. I felt trapped and held captive inside a body I no longer recognized.

It was always there, when I was playing with my daughter, when I went out on a date night with my husband, at family gatherings, at church. It followed me everywhere. I asked God every single day to deliver me from the pain.

In a fit of desperation one night, feeling overcome by it all, I screamed to my husband: "Where is HE? Where is GOD? Why is this happening to me?"

He grabbed me by my hand and brought me my Bible.

"Open it. Open it now."

Sobbing and hysterical, I opened straight to Psalm 73:23-6 (The Living Bible): "But even so, you love me! You are holding my right hand! You will keep on guiding me all my life with your wisdom and counsel; and afterwards receive me into the glories of heaven. Whom have I in heaven but you? And no one on earth as much as you! My health fails;

CHRONIC PAIN

my spirits droop, yet God remains! He is the strength of my heart; he is mine forever!"

I knew in that moment: He was right there with me. I felt His perfect peace settle on me and quiet all my doubts. The scripture fed my soul and I felt strengthened. I was able to regain my composure. Brett prayed for me and we cried together. God showed up every time for me. I was in pain, but He was there and so was my husband. I was devastated, but He was holding me. I was worn and weary, but He strengthened me.

In the worst throes of intense pain, I used to sit on my couch watching, "Jesus, He Lived Among Us" with my son. There is a part in the movie where a woman with a bleeding disorder touches the hem of Jesus's garment, and He says, "Who touched me?" because He knew healing power had gone out of him. (Mark 5:30)

The disciples thought this was a ridiculous question because since they were in a crowd, Jesus had brushed against many people and they were thinking, "Who hasn't touched you?"

But Jesus knew that someone had reached out to Him with faith; an expectancy to be healed by Him with just a touch of his clothing. The woman thought to herself, "If I can just touch the hem of his garment, I can be healed." And immediately, her bleeding stopped and she felt in her body that she was freed from her suffering. (Mark 5:29)

Her blood had been flowing out of her for twelve years, and it was as if her life was going away, flowing out of her ... until that day, when Jesus's life flowed in and healed her.

I would lie on the couch, hugging my son, crying tears of desperation to be healed, believing that if I could just touch Jesus's hem I, too, would be miraculously well again.

There was only one problem: Jesus was no longer physically walking around on the Earth.

However, I believed that Jesus was still very much alive, and the Bible tells us that with God, all things are possible. (Matthew 19:26)

So why couldn't I have an encounter with Him in modern times?

My faith had come out of the box, and I believed that He was limitless and started to press into His promises with childlike faith inspired by my son's relationship with Jesus. I needed a miracle, and I prayed daily to see Jesus, to experience an encounter that would change my life because I believed He could make it happen if it was in accordance with His will.

I decided that come what may, I was going to cling to Jesus and trust Him.

I felt like no one except my son, my daughter, and my husband who lived with me on a daily basis and saw me struggling to function – to clean the house, even somedays to sit upright – really understood a fraction of the condition I was fighting to endure. In general, I felt like most other people in my life really tried to be sympathetic but didn't understand the true depths of my hurting.

There were no words, I discovered, that could convey the depths and waves of all-consuming pain that ravaged my body in every moment. All the while, I looked perfectly fine on the outside.

I felt like I was constantly under a thick cloud of suspicions, cast in my direction by many close to me. But through this God took me to deeper levels in Him of understanding it was He who truly defines me and only He really understands. Why did I keep looking to people for validation about the physical pain I was experiencing? I wanted them to understand me, and to feel understood by them like I thought I was before I was in chronic pain; instead, I could see they never really saw me or understood me at all, not even in when I was in good health.

I saw the only one capable to understand me intimately enough to grasp the entirety of who I am is God. Not people.

CHAPTER 15

Italy

In August of 2018, I felt the Lord's prompting for me to get on Ancestry. I was confused by feeling led to go down this rabbit hole because I thought after I chose to forgive my biological father that was the happy ending to my story. That was the very best I could hope for: to forgive him and move on, and to do my best to try and accept what little I knew from my mother's version of events in regards to him, even if they didn't make sense or add up entirely.

But mostly, I still felt afraid that if I did search for him, he may hurt me or my mother – and I knew she certainly wouldn't approve of my actions.

I came to a fork in the road as I was deciding what to pursue: **Did I trust God or was I going to let fear limit me from moving forward?** I pushed past my fear, purchased a kit, sent it in, and anxiously waited for the results.

Two weeks before I received the results, Lincoln and I were on the way to meet my mother, sister, and my brother, who was in town at the time. As we started to pull into the diner, Lincoln said out of nowhere, "Mom, your biological father is up in heaven."

I was a puddle of tears and snot immediately. At this point, I did not know of his passing, and there's no way my son could have known, either. I had never entertained the thought that my biological father could possibly be in heaven due to the way my mother characterized him. But in that moment, I knew what Lincoln said was true. I just knew.

I felt comforted knowing that he was in heaven, and sad all at once. When I walked into the diner to meet my family, I couldn't hide that I was emotional, so I explained to them what had taken place. They were all in shock, but I noticed curiously my mom's face was more of a mix of shock and rage. She pursed her mouth and then forced a smile. Why was I getting her fake smile?

Confirmation of what Lincoln spoke came at the hands of a relative I connected with on the website, once my Ancestry results were available. I learned my biological father had indeed passed over a decade ago, and along with news of his passing went any hope I once had of connecting with him in this life.

I was reeling. Mourning and devastated, I called my mother to tell her the news, and she angrily spouted in a demanding tone: "WHY ARE YOU CRYING OVER HIM? HOW DARE YOU CRY OVER HIM!"

I was jolted and jarred by the hatred spreading to me through the phone and immediately went on guard. **I forgot, consumed by mourning and loss, that this was simply not about me. It was always about her.**

She reminded me like she had so many times in the past that I simply wasn't allowed to feel anything, ever, in regards to "that man." I made the mistake of thinking my mother would care about me going through such a horrific loss, but again, I was wrong. I did not find comfort. Instead, I found more criticism.

I rocked back and forth on the chair on my outside deck. I took in the crisp, autumn day and felt the warmth of the sun on my face as tears slowly rolled down my cheeks, a silent expression of the pain her words were inflicting.

"He was my biological father, and I never got a chance to meet him, Mom," I flatly replied, hoping she'd finally recognize that this matter concerned me too.

Noting my tone, she shot back at me even louder and angrier than her initial response. Sensing easy prey, it was as if my mother was a snake biting me with poisonous venom. I cried out in pain as she clamped down hard, hitting me with the force of her words.

It was more than I could bear – silently mourning the death of a man I'd prayed for and hoped to meet someday, burying him and the dream I'd had of meeting him, paired with my mother's contempt. It was more than I could take and I felt shattered.

I had looked to my mother, once again, to comfort me at a time when I desperately needed her to provide a soft spot for me to land. She denied me that: even in his death. She denied me the simple comfort of her shoulder. I knew, this was who she was and what she would do to me, but the truth was I never wanted to believe it about her. I had her on a pedestal, and no one was going to take her down, not even me.

I did my best to compose myself and asked, simply, "Mom, have you forgiven him?"

She paused, seemingly offended by my question, and I could tell it caught her off-guard. "Well, I'd never thought about it." And then she made an excuse to get off the phone.

Simultaneously, another blow hit me when my true ethnicity was revealed. I am:

33% England & Northwestern Europe

24% Germanic Europe

20% Scotland

8% Wales

7% Ireland

6% Sweden & Denmark

2% Norway

And ZERO percent Italian.

I used to dream of visiting Italy as a little girl, ever since my mother told me that was my father's ethnicity. For as long as I can remember, it was sprung on me in various ways, painfully peppered throughout my childhood and adulthood whenever she felt like speaking about it. She even cited a story several times where she personally overheard him speaking Italian on a phone call, with what she assumed to be his Mafia associates for confirmation.

I confronted my mother with my results, and she took no accountability. It was her reaction that was always the most disturbing; often times it was more upsetting than the shock and pain of catching her in yet another one of her confusing tall tales.

My mother failed to understand how much Italy mattered to me. I used to picture myself going on a gondola ride, enjoying various dishes, and taking in the scenery of a new and exciting exotic country. More than all of these, I longed to be connected in some way to my biological father, and the idea of visiting Italy gave me access to this hope because there was a bridge – an actual physical location – on this Earth where I could stand and feel connected to him. Italy was where he came from, and if I could hold onto anything certain, it was this fact: This concrete something that I knew about him to be true.

It turns out, Italy is someone else's dream. **Italy belongs to a little girl so desperate to be loved that she longed for a different country entirely, a place where she believed she could be loved.**

Italy will always be in my heart because I know it's where my little wounded girl's heart felt a connection. Someday, I'm going to take her on that gondola ride, and we will take in a sunrise together and watch it light up the beauty of the Italian architecture. We're going to indulge in all the homemade pasta dishes she dreamed about and laugh and reminisce together. We'll eat decadent desserts and drink fancy coffees at cafés. We will walk the streets together taking in the new sights.

And when it's time to leave, I'm going to say good-bye to her: the sweet child who longed to be loved. Whenever I think of her, I'll picture her there, smiling and laughing, playing and riding the gondolas, relishing in her long-anticipated dream finally becoming a reality ... she grew up and found love.

CHAPTER 16

Pain and Freedom

Soon after revelation of his death and the aftermath of the conversation with my mother, the pain was again significantly worse in my jaw. It was so tremendous I went to the emergency room.

Again, worse pain in my body was manifesting after an altercation with my mother. They could not help me, so I went to the dentist for imaging to rule out any dental issues. It was discovered that I would need a root canal on one of my molars. Following the procedure, I struggled for weeks with nerve spasms in my jaw and it felt like there were Fourth of July fireworks going off in my head.

I knew it was truly God that was helping me along because I was still traumatized by the image of scissors coming at me from having the tumor on my tongue removed. The sound of a dentist's drill at this point in time incited fear, and I cried as I had to endure yet another procedure when the dentist placed the crown in my mouth.

I could barely talk. I couldn't chew hard foods and was on a diet consisting of protein shakes during this time period. I spent mornings dragging my body out of bed and through the hallway, clinging to the railing for support as I made my descent down the stairs, biting my lips to keep from letting the agonizing, sheer pain raging through my body escape through my mouth.

More than the physical pain, though, was the agonizing heaviness that weighed me down my very worst days. The cyclical, seemingly unending torment of it all. I'd grit my teeth and muster up enough energy for some tasks, but mostly I'd cry, on these days where it was all crashing down on me. I'd feel the aching, throbbing intensity pulsating through me like an unwelcome intruder in my own body, violating me from the inside out.

Some days the pain would completely take over and those moments would linger, seemingly forever. It was like time stopped and stalled completely, and I'd feel like I might just be stuck like this for the rest of my time on Earth.

I read my Bible constantly, scouring the pages for answers. If no one on Earth could help me in my current state, then my only hope was going to be found in these pages. I needed answers.

I read the entire book of Job and wailed and begged God for an explanation. I called my mother that same evening and cried in desperation on the phone, sobbing to her. "Job got a messenger! I want a messenger! What is going on with me? I can't handle this pain, Mom. I can't handle it one minute longer!"

My mother was, as usual, not supportive and treated me like I was speaking crazy talk. She told me to calm down and acted put-off that I called her in the first place, despite my distraught state. I got off the phone with her further discouraged and feeling like I was in worse pain, again.

The next evening, on the night of Oct. 26, 2018, my son woke up and came downstairs to the main level, where Brett and I were seated and talking. He said, "Mom, someone whispered in my ear, 'Tell Mom,' and then I heard heaven's bells ringing. I think I have a message for you."

My mouth dropped open. Lincoln had no way to know that the previous day, I had asked God specifically for a messenger. Brett and I sat there, just looking at one another and at Lincoln.

"What's the message?" I asked.

Lincoln didn't know what it was, so we all bowed our heads and prayed.

Then Lincoln exclaimed, "I've got it!"

He said definitively, "I need to lie down first."

Then, as Brett and I looked on, his eyes began flickering and he spoke: "Your Mom can handle the pain. She thinks she is collapsing, but she isn't. The Devil is trying to get her, but she is doing a good job. Your Mom can handle the pain."

Lincoln's eyes stopped flickering, and he sat up. Brett and I exchanged frightened looks and I searched for paper to write down what Lincoln had just told me. I had a million questions. What just happened to my little boy that something literally took him over on the couch? Is this even real? Am I dreaming? The Devil? Why would he want to get me? Wait, he's actually real? The actual Devil is real?

When I was little, my mother would openly talk about demons and the devil with her mother and other family members when I was present. They seemed to label everything demonic. This was demonic. That was demonic. Everything is demonic all the time. It frightened, annoyed, and scared me so much, I was closed off completely to even talking about the Devil or anything related to him as an adult. I didn't even want to go there. Ever. I avoided talking about anything supernatural that I viewed in a negative manner, like the Devil, demons, and hell. I preferred to focus on Jesus and the more uplifting side of Christianity and be done with the rest.

Now I found myself eerily standing face-to-face with the harsh and unexpected reality that the Devil quite possibly could be very real, and also a plausible explanation for the pain I was experiencing. I couldn't just brush off the fact that my son randomly claimed to hear heaven's bells along with "Tell Mom" and then proceeded to go all creepy scary-movie-style on me with fluttering eyes and a message about the Devil a night after I had asked specifically for a messenger from God. Who was I that the Devil was going out of his way to take me down?

I didn't have much time to think about it, as the pain worsened so much following my most recent conversation with my mother that evening that I went to my nurse practitioner the following day. She suspected meningitis, so I was rushed immediately to the emergency room, where they gave me a spinal tap. They said if I did not submit to one, they would not admit me into the hospital to further investigate.

The results came back negative, and I was admitted into the hospital for further testing.

The cold, scary nights when I felt so incredibly alone were the worst. One evening, the nurse shared with me they suspected I may need neck surgery and were waiting on an MRI to come back to confirm, but it was a good possibility that I could be going to surgery the very next morning. Terrified and alone with the possible prognosis, I reached out to my mother to see if she'd come back to the hospital that night and stay with me.

"I'm going to cut hair right now, MacKenzie. No, I'm not coming."

I cried and begged her to care about me. I broke in a million pieces that night in the hospital room, alone. Having my own children at this point, I thought about if one of them was in the hospital. What would I have done in that situation? You would have had to drag me out of that room if my son or daughter was in the bed instead of me.

In that moment, all the red flags culminated and led me here: I knew something was broken in her, and it wasn't my fault. Caring for my own children helped me to see her inability to provide care for me.

I was feeling neglected and wondering if any of my friends truly cared because by the second day, only my friend Jenny and her husband, Ed, had stopped by to bring me flowers and say hello. I was in desperate need of support, especially for someone from my church to come and pray with me. I updated my social media, so everyone I was friends with from church was well aware of my condition, and I sent an email directly to the pastor of our church. I called Regina, who cited "hospital uncleanliness" as her reason for not visiting.

Social media greetings, text messages, and electronic well-wishes weren't cutting it for me on this occasion. Had this simply become our culture's way of feeling they had been there for someone, in lieu of showing up in person? Or was it that I simply hadn't made the close connections with others I thought I had? I determined it was probably a combination of both and decided to put deeper thought into the relationships I had established.

My sister and her husband did stop and see me a few times during the day while I was in the hospital. They took numerous CT scans and gave me a lot of painkiller medications. I was diagnosed with a condition called Myofascial Pain Syndrome. It's a disorder in which pressure on sensitive points in the muscles causes pain in seemingly unrelated body parts and often happens after repeated injury or muscle overuse.

I was released from the hospital after four days and three nights with more follow-up appointments scheduled with specialists. I made sure that no one could say I didn't try to reach out and ask for help while I was in the fight of my life. Despite how bad the pain felt, I kept bravely sharing my struggle with those who were willing to listen, at all costs to my reputation. I decided no matter how my story ended, I was going to speak out for those who felt silenced while walking through a mysterious chronic health battle.

CHAPTER 17

One Day at a Time

Home from the hospital, I felt groggy and disoriented from all of the medication. I would stand in the shower daily and weep and sob so the water would wash my tears away and wouldn't create such a mess in my bed and all over me. One really bad day in particular, I was crumpled up on the floor of the bathroom, naked and wailing. The pain was a level fifty on a scale of ten and it felt in those moments it was never going to let up. Rushing, condemning thoughts flooded me all at once.

"Just end it all."

"This will never get any better."

"You're going to be stuck like this."

"You can't handle this pain."

"You're a terrible mother, your kids deserve better."

The thoughts bombarded me, tore into me, and left me feeling helpless.

I could hear my children and my husband playing but didn't feel well enough to join in. I felt so guilty. I was living my life on the other side of the door, night after night, and felt like no one cared that I couldn't live my life except me.

A large bottle of Vicodin grabbed my attention. I waited until my husband left for work, grabbed the bottle, and seriously wondered if this would do the job. The thought that, "All of this will be over if you just take those pills" consoled me. I was desperate for relief. I wanted the misery to be over. I felt alone and misunderstood, that I'd fought so hard but was exhausted and at the end of my rope.

I looked at the pills and sobbed because I couldn't do it. The pain I felt of being trapped was crippling.

Afterwards, I felt taunted by the inability to take myself out, like even that was too hard for me.

"Don't be a coward! Now's your chance. If you take them, this will all end and you'll be free."

I'd hear the words, tempting me with death. They kept coming at me.

"Just take yourself out."

"You know it's the only thing that will end this."

The worst thoughts plagued me on the days that I was at my weakest. I battled and prayed to God with all my strength that they'd go away, that He'd make them stop, and I would find relief. When it came down to it, no matter how much pain I had to bear, I wasn't going to voluntarily leave my children.

My husband did his best to sympathize with my plight, but he was stretched, worn, tired, and weary. He was in charge of it all and working a full-time job. He comforted me when he could, but he himself was pulling from an empty well. He had the impossible task of trying to keep our family running and I was a mess.

I cried and cried. I begged God to help me. I prayed, I worshipped Him, and I pleaded with Him to please free me from it all. I noticed the more I praised and worshipped God, despite my pain, the more I would feel some relief from the intensity.

I was openly sharing about the pain I was in, but since I never had a solid explanation, for the most part I think people thought I was fine, since I was able to pull myself together to get out of the house.

"One day at a time" became my motto. I'd tell myself, "Just make it through the end of this day. Stay alive one more day."

When illness shook everything, I had held dear my whole life – money, success, prosperity and worldly possessions – I saw there was only emptiness to the dream I had built. I saw most of my relationships had proven shallow and were lacking in depth. I saw there weren't many people who were willing to sit and comfort me when everything got incredibly real; people evacuated my life like a tidal wave was coming and ran for shelter, leaving me to take the full impact on my own. When the wave hit, I got washed away with it, but I didn't stop fighting.

Even though I had been swept away, God offered me branches to grab a hold of; He offered me rest when I couldn't tread the water anymore. But, soon enough, the branch would break and I'd be swept along with the current, dragged through, gasping for breath. And just when I had no idea how I'd surface again, there He was, pulling me back out, setting me on solid ground.

I knew I wasn't the one getting myself out of the water. I knew I wasn't saving myself because I couldn't possibly do it on my own. I had no reserves in my tank. I had been completely emptied of everything I'd known to that point in my life. I understood that money, possessions, and people were all useless, and I became keenly aware I couldn't fight this battle with my usual arsenal of weapons.

This battle was different than all the others I'd faced previously. I was in the battle of my life, and I knew how much I needed God. He and only He could save me, and so I decided to let go.

I let the wave wash away everything I had known to that point. I let go of people. I let go of my reputation. I let go of money. I let go of my dreams and exchanged them for His. I let go of anything that was hindering me from Him, and He answered my prayers. Over and over and over again, God pulled me from the rushing water at the exact time I needed a breather. He'd refresh me, reassure me, encourage me, and then before I knew what happened, I was back in the water again, fighting for my life.

I was in new territory and sometimes the water raged at such a speed I was sure I was going to be submerged and not feel the sun on my face again. But no, this was not His plan. Each time, He'd step in. He'd save me.

I complained to God, "It feels like I only get back on my feet just to get knocked down again."

In response, I heard "Yes, but you're getting up much quicker now."

He was using the tremendous force of the tidal wave to train me for war.

I went and got a second opinion about the root canal I had done previously because it was still bothering me. Turns out the dentist who did my gold crown forgot to remove the cotton before sealing it. As a result, I would need another lengthy procedure to remove the leftover cotton. I felt like I could not catch a break, but simultaneously, everyone else was living their own lives oblivious to the pain I was now enduring on a daily basis.

My life continued to remain a blur of doctor appointments and pain. I was still seeing multiple specialists to help my back and the TMJ issues were ongoing. In addition, I was now seeing a rheumatologist, someone at the pain clinic, and a neurologist for terrible migraines. I was on heavy nerve medication, muscle relaxers, and Vicodin.

Regina began to get much more assertive in voicing her opinions about how I was handling my medical journey. She lectured me and wanted me to pursue more holistic remedies, and I often left our time spent together feeling shamed and confused. My husband started to notice that I'd come home in a frazzled state after meeting with her.

"Honey, do you see how unhappy you are after you hang out with her?" he'd ask me. "Why do you put up with her harsh criticism?"

I found myself apologizing to her constantly for my own medical journey – and buying more and more oils and products from her. My pain was now worsening after our interactions.

On social media, I was openly posting "health updates" about my recent diagnoses to keep everyone in the loop and to raise awareness for those like myself, engaged in mysterious chronic health battles. I had received a plethora of more diagnoses such as fibromyalgia (along with another corresponding prescription), white mass brain disease, and arthritis. I felt like a human lab rat. I'd start one medication, stop another; switch the dosage of this, up the dosage of that.

I was exhausted and suffering from feeling like everything was collapsing in around me. So many different opinions. There was what one doctor said, and then another would say something different. I was constantly suffering a variety of unpleasant side effects as a result. I prayed relentlessly that God would give me the strength to finally find the root cause of all of my pain.

My friendship with Regina made me feel like I couldn't do anything right, and I was a wreck most of the time because I had invested so much of myself – my heart, my love, my time – into our friendship. The last thing I wanted was trouble with friends and desperately wanted to feel supported. Instead, I found myself further emotionally and spiritually tormented at a time where I really needed kindness. And by a church friend, no less.

Little by little, I was watching Regina disappear before my very eyes, lost in her pursuit to be included by the popular crowd (women in leadership) at church. Where I once saw her as genuine and caring, **I was starting to see her as something more sinister: a social climber at church.**

I believe there is a fine line between educating yourself, putting measures in order that you think necessary for you and your family, and pushing your views on other people to a level that makes them feel berated for not taking your special brand of advice. Why did I value someone's friendship when it was clearly making me feel unworthy?

It suddenly started to click into place for me. My unhealthy relationship with my mother thrived on me being wrong and her being right. I was starting to understand that, as a Christian, I wasn't being called to label people as "good" or "bad" or their ideas as "wrong" or "right." Sure, I have my own personal set of beliefs, but even if they had a different set, I was being called not to a place of judgment, but to a place of loving others regardless of how they had decided to use their God-given free will.

God is the judge. Not people. I was used to submitting to someone else and foregoing my own thoughts about what I should be doing, or what I wanted, and replacing those with someone else's narrative, opinions, and advice about what I should be doing. I had bought into the right vs. wrong way. As I faced this pattern, I decided to start to shift it.

I got referred to a different specialist for my jaw. He confirmed I had been using the wrong appliance altogether and fitted me with a new one that focused on keeping my jaw stabilized.

As time wore on in 2019, my jaw was feeling better overall. I learned to get second opinions sooner rather than later – had I left the first specialist sooner, I could have found relief faster. Currently, I am in the final stages of my treatment with orthodontic care to align my teeth.

The results of an MRI came back in May with reports of a pituitary tumor. I got further testing and added a neurosurgeon to the list of specialists I was already visiting, but eventually it was ruled out as a source for the pain I had been experiencing.

This news was bittersweet because at this point, I wanted legitimacy to wash away the years of confusion sprawling across people's faces while I bravely struggled to describe what my journey had been. Why were people more interested in telling me what to do instead of offering to sit with me? Now, when I encounter someone walking through mysterious chronic pain, I simply listen and live in the moment with them without judging their journey, or giving my opinion unless they specifically ask me.

CHAPTER 18

Gold Crosses

Since I was attending so many medical appointments, I decided to look for the greater good I could accomplish instead of focusing on myself and my issues. When I was no longer my focus, I started to see the medical workers in the various offices differently. Some were very worn and weary, while others were upbeat, positive, and encouraging.

I started to notice a trend at my appointments with workers specifically wearing gold cross necklaces. Sometimes it would be someone at the front desk, or a nurse, or the doctor I had an appointment with that day. But the person wearing the cross would always end up being the one I connected with the most.

I started complimenting and encouraging staff at my appointments and I could see the surprise on their face when they read over my chart about my cheery disposition despite my circumstances.

I witnessed stranger after stranger open up and share sensitive, personal hurts they were currently working out on a daily basis. I saw the deep need for an empathetic ear extended well beyond myself. A mother struggling with the loss of her husband, an overwhelmed nurse with too much on her plate, and interacting with countless healthcare workers who took extra time to care about me were some of the highlights along this journey.

I was beginning to see the power I possessed in my own pain. I wasn't helpless and could still be of great use to others. Despite what I was going through, when I put others before my own concerns, amazing experiences happened over and over. I started to look forward to witnessing what God would do at my next appointment, instead of the dread I had been feeling previously. Simultaneously, through the bravery of their shared experiences, I knew I wasn't alone in my pain, and I felt comforted.

I also formed a habit of saying a prayer over the entire office staff when I sat down to wait to see the doctor. It gave me something else positive to direct my attention toward – and kept my focus off of myself and worrying over the appointment.

I may never know on Earth how God has chosen to work through my prayers, but I do frequently picture the day in heaven where I get to meet those whose lives were touched and enriched through the simple prayers of a woman choosing to put others first, despite her own pain. I was finding joy and purpose in unexpected places and learning more about my true calling and the person I was destined to become to help others.

I still pray, when I remember to do so, when I enter new venues, to this day. I ask God to help everyone in the room and to bless each person.

Beauty was all around me, even if I wasn't feeling well, and when I decided to immerse myself in His promises and in what He spoke over me, I was able to experience joy simultaneously as I walked in the pain. As a matter of fact, I saw I was able to live a fuller existence when I saw how meaningless things like possessions were when compared to anchoring myself in the foundation of God's truth and flowing from this new place of self-sacrificial love for others.

Relationships now took precedence above everything else because I saw they were the place I was finding true fulfillment and the source of true connection and contentment. I began reflecting and making a conscious effort in other areas of my life to give others the support I had been craving. I decided to be who I wanted in a friend, a mother, a sister, and a wife, and to reflect on my actions in these roles and decipher how I could improve and grow in these areas and further enrich my relationships with others.

My eyes were opened to the new opportunities I had missed previously to capitalize on improving various aspects of these relationships.

I realized the concept of "making time for God" was nonsensical – like, somehow, I had to manage a way to fit Him in. I felt humbled by how He infiltrated my life, and now I saw Him in everything and everyone, all around me, constantly. I couldn't NOT think about Him or not see Him, now that my chronic pain had given me a new hunger to seek Him and our relationship had become fluid.

I couldn't possibly make time for Him because He *is* time. He is in everything and everyone. I thought about how everything on the Earth, in its own unique way – the trees, the animals, the sky, even my own children – now taught me and pointed me to Him in some new, undiscovered way. He was in me and I in Him and we were one on this road together, and I became aware that all along, all throughout my life, it had always been this way. He had always been with me, reassuring me that everything was going to be okay.

Now I have the privilege of being aware of His full presence in my life. He alone is the reason I have made it to this point.

I had found the way out – Jesus had set up a table in the middle of my chaos. He met me here and He did not leave. He held my hand and showed me how to depend on Him for everything when I had nothing else. He showed me scriptures I needed exactly at the right time, or played a song for me when I needed a boost. He had a friend I'd been missing send me a text or call me out of the blue, just when I needed it. Every time I came to a place where I was worried, He calmed me. He showed me that I already had everything I needed because I had Him – and He was where my victory was found.

Even if nothing changed in my life, He had changed me through the pain. I felt an intimacy with the Lord that I had never known, and He changed me, even though my circumstances remained unchanged.

On July 5, 2019, at 8:44 p.m., my husband, son, and I were all outside on the deck. I grabbed my phone and started taking pictures of a phenomenal sunset. I'd never seen anything quite like it: The sun was hot pink and looked to be blazing.

As I shot pictures, suddenly an angel flew out of the hot pink, flaming sun. The three of us all saw him, and I captured a picture of him on my phone.

Lincoln shouted, "God sent me an angel for my birthday! God sent me an angel! Wow!"

My husband and I exchanged awestruck glances.

"That was an angel...." my husband trailed off.

Soon after, our next-door neighbor happened to step outside and Lincoln shouted over to him, "My birthday party is tomorrow, will you come?" Before I could say anything, he accepted the invite.

I grabbed my phone and looked through the shots I took once we went inside. I enlarged the picture of the angel – we could see facial details, wings, what appeared to be a halo, and a scroll in the process of being unrolled in his hand, above his right wing. I studied the image for hours that evening, wondering what this could mean.

What was written in the scroll? What is happening? I had a million unanswered questions, and I knew a search engine wouldn't be of much assistance in this case. I reached out to family and some friends sharing the image, asking what it could mean, but they too, had no answers.

I struggled to grapple with the events that had unfolded. Life had taken some pretty strange turns recently. My son was delivering me messages from God, the Devil was out to get me (apparently, he was real), there was an angel in our backyard, and I was still actively engaged in an all-encompassing unresolved pain battle as I prepared to have one hundred of our closest friends and family over to celebrate Lincoln's eighth birthday.

I had gone overboard with a "Super Mario" theme. Our house was decked out with balloons, a piñata, and water activities set up for the kids in the yard, including a Slip 'N Slide.

Our neighbor was one of the first to arrive, pointing out two stuffed animals he'd left sitting outside on the green Ameren electrical box that served as a divider between our yards. "You see those stuffed animals?" he asked my son.

Lincoln excitedly answered, "Yes!"

Our neighbor continued, "Well, they aren't for you."

And then he proceeded to walk inside my house. Lincoln looked let down and confused, and I was lost for words myself.

As the party continued, I could see our neighbor mingling and downing beer after beer. We had some Corona for our guests, but he was drinking most of them. I watched across the room as my friends and family members reacted to him with alarming expressions, removing themselves from his company, along with their children.

I was taking all of this in when a guest inquired, "What is he doing here?"

I replied, "He lives next door and Lincoln invited him last night."

The partygoer continued, "He is a schizophrenic with a history of violence."

I did not know what to do at this point. Soon, without saying anything, he walked right out the front door of my home.

The next day, I tried to wrap my head around the fact that we had invited a violent schizophrenic to our son's birthday party unknowingly. I went back outside, sat on the deck, and stared at the sky.

On July 7 at 8:44 p.m. (the same time the angel had appeared), there was a hot pink, dragon-shaped, winged figure in the sky. Again, I had my phone and captured the image. In the middle of the dragon was a brightly lit dead fish, and it appeared to be alternating with a skull. It was an ominous figure that creeped me out. I had never seen anything like it.

I didn't have time to digest one event before something else completely out of the norm was happening, yet again. What was going on? I could feel in my soul that something big was about to happen. The tension was mounting and there was something coming.

CHAPTER 19

The Encounter

The following Monday morning, Brett left for work and I was alone in the house. I was on the phone with my mother, speaking to her about my neighbor specifically, when there was a *bang, bang, bang* on my front door. I froze.

"Could it be him?" I whispered to my mom, terrified.

We have five small windows on both sides of our door, so I poked out to take a quick peek.

"YES! YES! It's him! Oh, Mom what do I do?"

Before I had time to really think, my doorbell began ringing over and over and over. I started to hyperventilate. He was pounding on the door so hard it sounded like it was going to cave in any minute.

Suddenly, I was transported back to another traumatic experience. I had lived together in an apartment for a few years with my best friend in our twenties. One day, around afternoon, I was lying on the couch in our living room watching TV and she was in her bedroom. Suddenly, there was loud banging on our door, so intense it was apparent the goal was to break down our door. Panicked, I ran and peeked through the window in her room to see the front door. I could clearly see two men, one facing outward, appearing to be the lookout for other people passing-by, and the other kicking, hitting, and doing his best to knock down our door.

We exchanged terrified glances and I started screaming, "Get away from our door! We're calling 911!"

And that's exactly what we did. The banging stopped and they left. After the incident, my roommate said, "Oh my gosh, Kenzie."

I looked over and realized that we had just locked the door only minutes before they'd gotten there.

"If I hadn't locked it," she said, "they would have been in the apartment."

We stood there in awe of how she had saved us by locking that door.

"MacKenzie! MacKenzie! Calm down. My goodness. Breathe," I heard as I was pulled back into the present moment. The banging continued and I screamed, terrified and aware that the man attempting to break down my door was not mentally well.

"I'm calling 911! I have to go, Mom."

I hung up and called the police. They arrived within minutes. When they got to my house, my neighbor had left temporarily, so I let one of the cops inside and shut the door behind him without locking it, assuming I was safe since the cops were on the scene.

I was wrong.

To my horror, my neighbor came into my home, ran around the cop, and lunged at me. I screamed and ran as the cop escorted him out to the front of the yard. The cops filed a report but did not arrest him. He was warned to keep away from our home and went back into his house next door.

We didn't have a security system at the time, so I was at a loss. What was I supposed to do now? Hope he didn't try to come back? Who was going to make sure my family was safe? I guess I was to hope for the best.

It was in these moments my eyes were opened to the fact that law enforcement really couldn't keep me and my family safe. I could only rely on God. I also felt great sympathy for my neighbor. It was evident he was hurting and in need of help. It felt like a tragic, hopeless situation.

THE ENCOUNTER

I didn't get any sleep that night, and neither did my husband due to me feeling more afraid than I have ever felt in my life.

On Tuesday, July 9, 2019, I was beyond exhausted. My nerves were frazzled and I was terrified to leave my house. I could see our neighbor when I looked out the window, walking around with a beer in one hand and a cigarette in the other. We also made arrangements to get a security system installed as soon as possible.

I heard my doorbell ringing again relentlessly, and sure enough, my neighbor was back. He shook the door handle again and attempted to get inside. It was evident he needed the kind of help that I was not qualified to give, and I was at a loss as to what the right solution was in this situation.

There used to be a mental wellness facility in Peoria called Zeller Mental Health Center some time ago, but it had been torn down. Where was my neighbor supposed to go to get the help he needed to get better? He was as much a victim as I was in this scenario. I called the cops again to file another report.

That night, I laid my head on the pillow and prayed to God for comfort and reassurance in the midst of a scary situation. In the early morning hours, I had an encounter with Jesus that changed my life.

Up to this point, I had dreams that felt more real than reality, but I had never experienced a supernatural visitation while I was wide awake.

My eyes have always been terrible; I'm a -8.50 in both eyes, meaning I can't make out objects without my glasses. However, I could see everything Jesus was showing me with crystal-clear precision, more magnificently vivid than the very best LED TV could offer.

The first thing I saw was a sparkling, breathtakingly gorgeous, ruby-red downward death spiral. It was alive, shimmering and moving, but encrusted on the outside of the spiral were alternating dead fish and skulls with crossbones (similar to the dragon I had seen in the sky earlier). Suddenly, a small, supernatural television appeared. There was a backdrop of the most beautiful night sky with twinkling stars that looked so real they were breathing. I watched as the same red downward death spiral was now standing next to Jesus. Jesus was smiling, and He gently tapped the spiral to grab its attention, and then He laid down and closed His eyes. He rose again, opening His eyes, extending His arms, and a big smile danced across His face. He was reminding the spiral about how He overcame death through the resurrection. I gasped, celebrated, and shouted, "No way!"

I could not believe what I was seeing, but I was simultaneously terrified and couldn't believe this was happening.

He also showed me a stunning, ruby-encrusted butterfly in a brilliant deep, sparkling red, with me riding it against the backdrop of the night sky. Jesus was alongside the butterfly and I noticed the wings didn't move flatly, up and down. Instead, this butterfly's wings were completely mobile and did more of a wave action when it flew. It was spectacular and rich with dimension.

When we reached the top of the night sky, suddenly, the butterfly transformed into an eagle with me riding on the top and flew out of the view. At one point, I was standing face-to-face with Jesus and could see into His eyes. He also showed me himself standing at a chalkboard, and Nevada and her baby girl (my future granddaughter).

The color, richness, and clarity of the visions was crystal clear and sharp. In contrast, I find even the most spectacular scenery in the daily world in which we exist dull and out of focus. It's inscribed in my memory, like a part of me now, and I'll always treasure the unforgettable early hours of the July 10, 2019, visitation when I met Jesus in my bedroom.

I did not include every detail of my encounter that night here and don't know if I'll ever understand everything that happened, but I have gained more insights as time has passed.

My health improved greatly overnight, and I did not struggle with the extreme degree of exhaustion and pain as I had previously. I would catch Brett staring at me from time to time, with an expression I hadn't seen before: wonder. He knew something was very different with me and celebrated my newly improved health.

CHAPTER 20

True Peace

I now heard a kind, gentle voice. I recognized it and knew I had heard it here and there before, but now it was more prominent, clearer and louder.

"I love you."

"You're doing a great job."

"I'm with you and I won't leave you."

The voice spoke into my soul and nourished and encouraged me. I no longer heard things like, "You really messed this up" and "You'll never feel better" and "You should quit now; there's no point." Those thoughts had been silenced, and instead, I had renewed energy and a revived spirit. I felt more whole, like something inside me had been restored and healed.

My entire perception of Jesus changed following this encounter. How I had pictured Him and envisioned Him was gentler, passive and loving ... but a battle commander? No. I had never thought of Jesus as a superhero waging war, but that's exactly who I met that night.

When His gaze met mine, it was clear He had shown up to handle business. His eyes were blazing with fire full of fierce determination and power that literally took my breath away. He was poised and confident, and it was evident He came to war for me with violent, all-consuming, passionate love. Matthew 10:34 tells us that Jesus "did not come to bring peace to the Earth; but a sword."

A sword of love – to war with love. It is so much easier to hate than to love, to hold something against someone than to choose to forgive and love them. **Hate is always the clearer, easier option, but to decide that no matter the cost you will walk in love and forgiveness is not the passive, easier option. Love is an act of war demanding a true warrior mentality.**

I believe by showing me riding a butterfly that transitioned into an eagle, that meant He is going to continue to take me from glory to glory. The butterfly signified that I was a new creation in Him. From 2 Corinthians 5:17 ESV, "Therefore, if anyone is in Christ, he is a new creation. The old has passed away; behold, the new has come."

The eagle represented my revitalized strength physically, emotionally, mentally, and spiritually. From Isaiah 40:31 KJV, "But they that wait upon the Lord shall renew their strength; they shall mount up with wings as eagles; they shall run, and not be weary; and they shall walk, and not faint."

Jesus was about to teach me brutal truths about myself and to walk me through a painful purification process purging old habits, lies, and thought processes. I was about to come face-to-face with my own sexual abuse for the first time, trauma I had long forgotten and buried.

In the movie *The Matrix*, Neo was presented two pills by Morpheus. Morpheus says, "You take the blue pill … the story ends, you wake up in your bed and believe whatever you want to believe. You take the red pill … you stay in Wonderland, and I show you how deep the rabbit hole goes."

Like Neo in *The Matrix*, I had opted for the red pill, the one representing the truth no matter the consequences of going down the rabbit hole, and I was about to go down a path of deep self-discovery.

I was no longer terrified of my neighbor or anything concerning him after that night because I felt at peace regarding our safety. I felt His protection over me and my family. I felt prompted to ask family and friends to pray that the neighbor would be moved to a new location; preferably one where he could get the help he clearly needed.

A few weeks later and without any new incidents, our doorbell rang one evening. It was our neighbor. My stomach flip-flopped, hoping all would be well. My husband made the decision to answer the door. He stepped outside with our neighbor, closed the door, and walked him to the sidewalk.

Before he could speak, our neighbor said, "I just wanted to stop by and tell you that I am going to be moving."

A couple of weeks later, he came back and asked my husband for help moving a dresser and a bed out of his home. Brett agreed to help him.

We thanked God that He answered our prayers, and that was the last time we saw our neighbor to date. I hope and pray he has gotten the help he needed. I couldn't help but feel there was more we could be doing in our community to help mentally ill people like my neighbor.

After my encounter, God told me "It's time to write. You're a writer. Write three pages a day."

For a month, I heard this daily and would laugh at the thought. Me? A writer? I have no formal training and have never written anything besides in my diary from time to time throughout the years. Actually, it's my husband who has his master's degree in journalism. If anyone was going to write anything in our home, shouldn't it be him?

I spent a month grappling with what I was hearing and coming up with excuses why I wasn't a writer. By mid-August, I had come to the end of my excuses as to why I shouldn't write and decided to comply with the request, even though I had no idea what I was writing about at the time and seriously doubted my own capabilities.

Simultaneously, I was pinching myself and swept up in a pretty consistent state of awe at the encounter I had with Jesus. I was in total shock of what had happened that night, and also what I was seeing each night since the encounter. A totally new supernatural realm had opened up since the night of his visit, and I was grappling to understand what I was seeing with my own eyes now each night as I lay in bed.

I watched epic battles take place night after night. I could see what appeared to be angels moving at lightning speed. This realm felt familiar to me and ancient at the same time. I'd take my hands and wave them in front of my face to see if anything happened. I'd close my eyes, and I could still see the realm. I noted it didn't matter if my eyes were open or closed. I was watching it either way and again, I didn't need my glasses to see perfectly.

I would say, "How is this happening? What am I supposed to do here? Why am I seeing this?" Every time I stopped to think about seeing Jesus, a huge smile welled up in my soul. I noticed how time flew by now, where before it seemed to be at a never-ending standstill. Simultaneously, I grappled to understand and interpret the events of the encounter.

Things started to shift for me quickly when I excitedly shared with family and a couple church friends. Ivy, now married and a pastor at her own church in Peoria, responded hastily with, "That's just not possible. The Bible tells us that Jesus is seated in heaven at the right hand of God."

It never crossed my mind that someone who claimed to believe in Jesus wouldn't believe I had seen Him.

Surprisingly, at first, my mother said she believed me and seemed excited. But as time went on, she started to change her mind, and confessed to me on the phone one day, "Well, I'm going to be honest, I'm on the fence about whether to believe you or not. I'll wait and see if I believe you saw Jesus and judge you by your fruit."

She had put me on notice and now I felt like my behavior and actions must be more perfect, by her standards. However, I was still unperfect MacKenzie, even though the encounter had changed me in ways I was still discovering and continue to uncover to this day.

I see now I was trying to prove something that I never could, and I was seeking the approval of others even over my precious encounter with Jesus. Galatians 1:10 (NIV) asks, "Am I now trying to win the approval of human beings, or of God? Or am I trying to please people? If I were still trying to please people, I would not be a servant of Christ."

The truth is, I can't prove to anyone that I saw Him that night. However, it devastated me originally when people, especially Christians, did not believe me, especially those who seemingly knew me best and knew how I'd been struggling terribly with my health. Why wouldn't they rejoice that I was feeling better? I had never claimed to experience anything like this before, and what possible reason would I have to make up this encounter? Was I putting Jesus first here, or my pride and reputation? Was I going to let what anyone else had to say about something I know had happened devalue it or make it not real?

No.

The encounter initiated a humbling process of exposing and ripping away, piece by piece, how I had gone to great lengths to please people first, instead of God.

CHAPTER 21

Releasing the Excess

I would describe my experience at the church during this time like fire.

On one hand, it burned me and further cemented a lot of the views I already possessed about church. Through my friendship with Regina and my experience at The Well, I felt like personal agendas such as promoting a business or friendship or being the most liked took precedence and detracted from the powerful, self-sacrificing message that is Jesus and the Gospel.

On the other hand, the experience warmed me by giving me an important key in my journey to help unlock some healing with forgiveness. I got burned by friendships and church, but in the burning and intense hurting, I was learning some important truths about myself and about what I was prioritizing and valuing. **God was using this fire to refine and purify me from relationships and places I aligned with that weren't for me anymore.**

I discovered that living with His hand guiding me wasn't as hard when I put aside my circumstances and people's opinions of me: the excess. When I focus on Him and offer myself to do His will on the Earth and pray for His kingdom come, then I am truly one with God and find such peace and contentment in His arms. When I let the world back in to infiltrate me in a weak moment, anger bubbles to the surface, or I'm frustrated and mad, my joy and my peace are gone. I make sure to give those emotions to the Lord and ask Him to "take me higher." **I want to fly higher and be with Him, not dragged down by my circumstances and by emotions.** I want to reside with Him, trusting Him fully. From Jeremiah 29:11 (NIV)

"For I know the plans I have for you," declares the Lord "plans to prosper you and not harm you, plans to give you a hope and a future."

When I read His word and refuse to step off of His promises over my life no matter what I am faced with here, heaven is enacted on my behalf. God can only move in our lives to the extent that we are believing Him to move, to the extent that our personal faith in Him will allow. Do we have big faith in God? Do we expect Him to be able to do what He says in our lives, meaning ANYTHING IS POSSIBLE WITH GOD?

From Mark 9:23 (NIV) "If you can?" said Jesus. "Everything is possible for one who believes."

I have rested on this promise solidly and I have seen incredible things. My eyes have also been opened through seeing Jesus and sharing my encounter to see how many Christians truly have God in a box, standing trapped inside along with a list they have assigned to Him about the things they believe He can and cannot do. I learned to stop taking rejection of my experience personally because it wasn't about me in the first place. It's always been about Him.

I've been called to write about my experience and leave it where it lies, regardless of other people's thoughts, criticism, or judgments. I'm grateful He's given me the wisdom to seek Him first and has strengthened me by breaking through the ties I had to the opinions of others.

I saw I had to stop letting what other people think hold me back from stepping into my destiny. Ephesians 1:11 (TPT) tells us, "Before we were even born, he gave us our destiny; that we could fulfill the plan of God who always accomplishes every purpose and plan in his heart."

He has a destiny for each one of us, and to truly walk with Him, we must pray and pursue His will above our own because that is where true joy, love, and contentment are found: when we fit into the will He has for our lives. When we are pleasing God, the rest will be added to us.

From Luke 12:31 (NIV) "But seek His kingdom and these things will be given to you as well."

RELEASING THE EXCESS

When we pursue Him at all costs to ourselves, He purifies us in that process. When we truly place Him and His kingdom and what He is asking us to do above money, above people, above jobs, above our own wants, above our opinions, above our own ideas, and above the world's expectation of us, heaven is unleashed in our lives! When we throw away the world's way of doing things and ferociously stand on His word and His promises while being done with the rest, He invades our lives!

I want to be an example of God's miraculous power being made manifest in my life, so I will let NOTHING and NO ONE stand in the way of His first-place position in my life. I want, above all else, for HIS WILL to be done, so I'm fiercely pursuing Him and asking Him to tell me what to do next.

God has been equipping me to step into my destiny by speaking to me along this journey that He is teaching me to "master my emotions." I've been praying into that and asking for more tools to show me what, exactly, mastering my emotions looks like in His terms.

I have discovered the key is to know exactly who I am so well that no one else can touch my character or who I am, even if they believe the exact opposite. The truth is I have no control over someone else's opinion of who I am, and each person has the free will to think whatever it is he or she wants to think. I needed to fully accept I am powerless to change anyone's narratives about me, my character, my life, or how I live my life to truly move forward.

Throughout this process, I heard the words, "Stay in your own lane, MacKenzie." I found freedom in those words by practicing and staying intentional about focusing on controlling my own thoughts, behavior, and reactions.

When I understood the simple truth that I only had control over my own thoughts and actions, I could be done exerting my energy to think about what others thought and could stop letting it invade my space. I released the excess by embracing the realization that I am not accountable for others' behavior. I laid down thinking about what they were saying, thinking, acting on, or doing where it concerned me because I realized, at the end of the day, none of what they think about me actually defines me. Yes, hearing harsh words or criticisms about who someone believes me to be hurts and I do have an emotional response in the moment, but through God, I do have the power to realize who He says I am and claim His authority in the situation, and to respond from a place of knowing myself instead of a place of hurt.

I am who God says I am; not anyone else. When I act from this new, solidified foundation, my feelings may be hurt here and there, but ultimately, I will never fall. Therein lies the power to overcome any and all circumstances. **I am the domino that will not fall because He is holding me up, regardless of who crashes into me.**

Destiny is more than simply a concept found in *Star Wars* or *The Lord of the Rings*. It has an applicability to your life right now! God designed our lives and our destinies to be an adventure lived in community with Him and one another. I love Proverbs 20:24 (TPT), which explains, "It is the Lord who directs your life, for each step you take is ordained by God to bring you closer to your destiny. So much of your life, then remains a mystery!"

The more we embrace destiny as an applicable concept for us, for right now, the more we are able to seek God in the mystery and explore – and, as a result, fall in love with the life He has given us because it transitions to a passionate, purposeful adventure full of miracles. One day at a time culminates and as you continue to pioneer living in the moment and trust God, your destiny is uncovered and revealed.

The more I thought and prayed about my destiny, the more I kept circling back to Chloe. I made a promise to her that the abortion would not be in vain. As I continued to write, I knew He was reminding me of the promise and giving me the blueprints to make good on my word. He was imprinting a deep yearning in my soul to help young women like myself, faced with an impossible decision and not having anyone to turn to for support.

I was not personally aware that I made the decision to have an abortion in a state of normalized and unrealized trauma, and completely unaware of my own state of mind. I wanted to go back for myself by finding a way to help other women understand how the various aspects of their own story factor into the decision regarding their pregnancy, help them to heal from trauma, and to feel empowered to make the best choice.

CHAPTER 22

Chloe's House

In my own experiences, when I tried to speak about abortion, I was surprised to discover that most of the time, the person I was speaking to couldn't get past the shock that I was openly discussing it with them to even partake in a meaningful conversation about the matter. It's hard enough to bring up the topic of abortion in general, but to go in one step further and let someone know you've actually had one is practically unheard of ... yet millions of women have had an abortion, including me.

Still, we don't feel comfortable enough to talk about it openly. The unspoken truth about getting an abortion is you don't tell anyone that you ever went and had an abortion for a reason. Mostly, that is because it would very possibly make the person you're sharing with uncomfortable, and they could possibly judge you. Simply by the sheer number of abortions performed, we know our neighbors, our sisters, our friends, even this author, have had an abortion. Why are we doing women like myself such a disservice societally by stigmatizing and shaming them with uncomfortableness when they choose to share their experiences?

I'm done with shame. It can't touch me anymore, so I will use my voice and speak out about my own personal experience in hopes that it will free another woman to feel she can do the same. What if we all decided to unite and be PRO-WOMAN? In light of Roe vs. Wade being overturned and the division that is spreading rampantly throughout our society on both sides regarding the verdict, it's beyond time to take our heated personal opinions about what we think pregnant women should or should not do and shelve them to help emotionally support the actual pregnant women who are tasked with making the permanent choice amidst the chaos this decision has unleashed about how to proceed with their pregnancy. We need to provide a place now, more than ever, where women can learn about and explore their options at a state level free from stigma, judgment, shame, and everyone else's ideas of what they should or should not do. We need a place where they can learn how the decision to overturn Roe vs. Wade impacts them personally in their state. It's time we put these women first and gave them a platform to be heard, valued, and respected, independent of the decision they choose and separate from the ravaging debate now surrounding their pregnancy and personal decision.

The main reason I am stepping out and sharing my story is because I want to start a nonprofit organization for women called Chloe's House. Chloe is Greek for "green sprout; the name of growth and discovery" and also means "blooming" and "fertility." The name also appears in the New Testament, in First Corinthians 1:11 in the context of "the house of Chloe," a leading early Christian woman in Corinth, Greece.

I'd like pregnant women who are investigating their options to be aligned and connected with certified therapists to speak to about their upbringing, their background, and their life experiences free of cost. The professionals can illuminate how all of these factors help to formulate their unique perspective and how the totality of it all has an impact on the decision they are making. It is my hope that through further exploring their own lived experiences with a therapist, women can get a more well-rounded idea of how their relationships with their mother, their father, and other family members contribute to forming their own perception about how they view motherhood, pregnancy, abortion, giving birth, and adoption.

We are each unique and have had our own journey specific to us in terms of pregnancy. I want this to be a place where each woman is met where she is at in her journey, listened to, and respected for the human being she is, regardless of her opinions or viewpoints. We each have different experiences that have helped mold and shape and make us into the person we are, and I think we each possess a valuable piece of information or knowledge to help someone else. And I believe we ourselves are helped and healed in the process, when we come together in a spirit of sharing and openness with one another.

Chloe's House will serve as a respite away from the opinions of the rest of the world not currently personally facing the choice regarding the heated, embroiled battle at the forefront of the decision to overturn Roe vs. Wade. It will be specifically focused on the women who are personally facing this decision apart from many who are weighing in with little to no personal experience walking out a pregnancy. This will also serve as a place of healing for women like me who have chosen an option they wished they wouldn't have chosen, but are able to come and find other women to lean on and therapists to talk to. I had no one to guide me through the hardest time in my life, so I want this to be the place I wished I could go to, to find out what's next, free of judgment.

I know Chloe's House won't be perfect, but neither is this world. Neither are circumstances. Neither am I. At the heart of my organization will be a burning desire and passion to help women have the ability and access to information, resources, therapy, and testimonies about various decisions other women have made, and how those choices have personally impacted them. I believe each woman deserves to have a voice, no matter her story, no matter where she is at, no matter what she believes. I envision a place where taboo conversations ruled too risky, too uncomfortable to discuss in society's typical places, can take place freely. **Chloe's House will take women's secret, silent pain and struggles off mute and give them back their voices.**

I want this to be a place where a woman can stand up, share her own experience and feelings, and discuss what she learned, while realizing that because it is her experience, it may not be the same for someone else. I realize that just because I regret my abortion, someone else might not. I realize their outcome, situation, and experience could be totally different from mine. But I still want her to have a voice. I still want her to feel she can speak about a decision she made, although she may feel completely different than I do because we are not the same person. My opinion and point of view are simply the culmination of the years and experiences I have uniquely lived thus far in my journey, so I do not expect anyone else to have an identical outlook.

I think our differences are what make us so spectacular. **We don't have to walk alone; we can walk together even if we are different.** We can come together and help one another grow, learn, and feel supported, simply by opening up and sharing our personal experiences.

I want to have ongoing open seminars for pregnant women considering their options to hear testimonies like mine. What does the decision to abort look like five years, ten years, twenty years down the road? **I want to book women to speak and share from all walks of life with all kinds of lived experiences, and choices made and the impact of that decision on their lives.** I want the woman who gave up her baby for adoption to share about the process, about how she felt, about how she feels now, and the same for the woman who chose to keep her baby and how she feels.

Each speaker can provide a fresh, personalized viewpoint of a different option she made and how it impacted her life. By listening to various women share a variety of experiences and choices, it is my hope the pregnant woman facing her own choice will feel more prepared and educated to decide what is best for her.

I'm grateful for friends like Regina, and for my mother because I believe they were used as sparks to ignite a truth now burning inside me: I have a voice and I deserve to be heard too. **Regardless of how others treat me, my voice matters.** What people think about my voice is their opinion, but that doesn't mean what I think or have to say is unimportant.

I am not going to let what other people think of me define me, stifle my voice, or determine how I will go about living my life. I get to decide independent of what people think about me or my voice. **My passion for Chloe's House is that it will serve as a platform for many women to feel heard, valued, and seen, and to know that their voice matters – to take back the narrative from the politicians, from our society, and stand united to write a new one together.**

Mine is just one of many, many stories out there. Regardless of what you think about me, my voice, or this writing, I put myself out here in hopes that I can spark the truth inside you too. Your voice is important, regardless of what anyone else thinks or says about it. It's yours. No one gets to define your story. You get to decide how and if you want to use it.

I also want Chloe's House to serve as a resource for people like another of my neighbors, to help positively further a cause they clearly feel so passionately driven to support. When we first moved into our new house, she had a huge sign in her front yard that said, "Abortion is Murder." Each time I left my home and saw it, I felt like a dagger was piercing my soul. The sign triggered me as I remembered the events that preceded my own abortion.

I know this woman a bit personally, and I can tell you it was not her intent to hurt me, but still, she did. When I see bumper stickers with a "murder" slogan, what I feel and have felt is more hate, more condemnation, more stones being flung my way. But now, mostly, I feel overwhelming sadness because I know there's a better way.

What if, instead, we all stopped arguing and collectively put our energy and resources toward a cause that could directly help the pregnant women regardless of our personal viewpoints?

In faith, trust and believe that God will prevail over the lives of the women coming to Chloe's House. God has gifted each one of us with free will and the ability to decide how we want to live our lives. He has called me to step into the trenches and love those who are battling regardless of political stance, personal beliefs, or affiliation. God has called us to love everyone. If you feel the same, join me to help make Chloe's House a reality. You can find out how to take the next step and get involved by visiting my website: https://www.mackenziekaynelson.com.

CHAPTER 23

The Other Side

This woman I am on the other side of processing and healing from my past is a different person from the woman who made the decision to abort that day at the clinic.

I was told that the abortion was a simple procedure and an end to my predicament, but for me, that didn't turn out to be the case. There is a condition referred to as Post Abortion Stress Syndrome (PASS), but the term has not been accepted by the American Psychiatric Association or the American Psychological Association. Symptoms of this syndrome include depression, anxiety, guilt, sadness, and regret following abortion. According to H3Helpline.org, the symptoms described in PASS are similar to the symptoms of Post-Traumatic Stress Disorder (PTSD). Many women and men experience heightened feelings of depression or anxiety at anniversary months of either the abortion procedure or the proposed birthdate of the aborted child. Unfortunately, many medical and mental-health professionals fail to recognize the painful aftermath of an abortion as an actual condition, making it difficult to feel heard or understood.

I believe there aren't enough of us stepping forward and speaking out openly about the very real pain we have suffered due to the stigma and shame surrounding abortion. If you are a woman who is or has suffered from PASS, I encourage you step out of the shame and speak up so other women who are considering an abortion can be informed of the very real possibility that they, too, might suffer from PASS following their procedure. As a result of our shared voices, it is my hope that the medical community will respond by taking PASS more seriously and legitimize and acknowledge the syndrome publicly.

I suffered immense trauma as a result of my decision, but I understand now that God works everything for His good. And I have found healing and hope on the other side.

Committed to the new assignment God had given me following the encounter, I kept writing three pages a day, no matter what my day brought. Left without a church to attend, I prayed and asked God what to do. I felt the Lord prompting me to go and support my sister and brother-in-law in their endeavors with the new church they pastored.

Clearly, my sister had made it known she did not believe me and my experience with Jesus, and I swallowed a lot of pride to go where I felt the Lord was sending me and my family. I was confused, but I knew what I was hearing and followed through, and started attending and tithing at her church.

There were around twenty members at most in attendance on Sundays, a congregation that was also comprised of my mother, grandmother, and one of my aunts. I did my best and offered to assist in any way I could, including donating some items from our home and trying to start up a program at the church to assist members who were in need. But I was quickly rebuffed and put on the back burner.

My sister's demeanor and attitude toward me made me feel unwelcome as the months progressed, and we decided to leave.

My mother didn't see our choice to depart from my sister's church as bearing "good fruit" (although she, too, has since departed from my sister's church). My decision to continue to write my book was starting to raise questions as well.

In October of 2019, my husband went to Las Vegas for a work convention. I asked my mother if she would come over and stay one of the nights with us, and she agreed. I was making dinner for us, and as I drained the pasta, my mother casually took a swing at me.

"You know, Lincoln is angry, just like you were."

I felt a strange feeling come over me and something fierce rising up inside.

"No, he's actually a very kind, sweet child. He loves Jesus, is a fantastic son, gets straight A's, has great friends, and gets along well with his sister. He isn't angry at all."

I could tell she was taken aback at my strong stand in opposition to her words. She started to question my book and what I had written that day. I happened to be writing the story about my dad moving my mattress out of the house, and I laughed as I started to share, remembering the mattress flying off his truck.

As I started the story, I was interrupted before I even got to the funny part by her gaslighting me and declaring, "That's not what happened at all!"

But I was done letting her truth overwrite mine. I confronted her with her own behavior and words regarding several scenarios from my past, where she had treated me poorly.

Then she left and slammed the door.

When we let fear drive the bus, it tends to drive us straight into the thing we are the most afraid of becoming.

Following this confrontation, I thought long and hard about quitting writing and deeply questioned my new mission. In hindsight, I think the little things I started to stand up for sparked some of the worst treatment towards me because they were threatening my mother's reign over my life. If I wasn't submitting to her control, that meant I didn't love her, and so she felt more and more threatened, especially due to my defiant act of getting on Ancestry.

God was calling me and I was listening, pressing in, reading scripture, doing every single thing He asked, and leaning on Him for help and support, instead of placing that first call to my mother, as I used to do. She knew she was losing control.

Other family members believed me to be some kind of amazing actress, I suppose, in their presence. I wonder how many times they must have felt the conflict rising in them: what they heard secondhand about me from my mother and sometimes my sister, and how they perceived me themselves. The two were always butting up against each other, and I could feel the conflict rising in them, and I received the backlash for it.

The harsh reality that so many, including myself, struggle to face is that not all mothers love their daughters.

As a result, no one could hear or see the real me. They could never invest in me with their hearts and they could never feel at home with me, or I with them. My mother had deprived and robbed me and the other members of our family of making the true connection with one another that we each longed for, simply so she could seize ultimate control.

If I would have agreed with my mother on that October night about her angry assessment of my son, I would have given her my blessing to treat my son the same way she treated me. I believe since she felt threatened by her loss of control over my life, she was upping the stakes, and trying to make his emotional abuse a team effort – bringing me in on the same game she had been using to manipulate me. In a desperate attempt to regain control, she used my son as leverage.

She showed her hand that evening by underestimating the fierce love I had for Lincoln because she did not have it for me. In hindsight, I look back and see this as the night where I took my final stand against the unjust treatment. This was the night where I said, "No. Not with my children. It all ends here."

CHAPTER 24

Life Without Mother

I was devastated to try and walk out my life without my mother, but I knew if I continued to contact her, my children and I would have to pay a price. Her love always cost something.

Grief is messy and complicated, and it hit in unrelenting torrents when I was least expecting it, especially as I approached my first holiday season without my mother and extended family. I wanted to celebrate the holidays and appreciate all the blessings in my life – amazing in-laws, a wonderful husband, two healthy, fantastic kids I adore – but grief can be deceptively tricky.

It snuck up on me while going on our annual Nelson tradition to Lou's Drive Inn, where a Christmas tree farm is stocked with beautiful, live trees for us to pick out each year. I was overwhelmed by the impending doom of celebrating Christmas without my extended family. I was paralyzed by the reality that things may never be the same again.

I remember feeling aware that my grandfather was getting older and had the thought that this could very well be his last holiday. In hindsight, I know the Lord put that thought into my head.

Still, I decided I couldn't let my kids walk into her house and hug her like how she spoke to them and to me was okay. I didn't want my children to be confused about appropriate behavior from adults, and they did not feel comfortable attending.

I noticed the old physical pain starting to flare up again as I faced this new, uncertain reality without my family. I was struggling with extreme fatigue again and I didn't want to do anything. I wanted to curl up in a ball and hide away from the pain and pretend like this wasn't happening.

I felt like I had lost an arm and a leg and was relearning how to navigate my life without the necessary appendages. Since my mother, sister, brother, grandmother, and other family members were still very much alive and well in the world, I was grieving and mourning my losses again, in total silence.

I was mourning the repetitive loss of trying so hard to please them, doing everything to win them over, grasping and begging for their love. No matter how many eggshells I managed to walk on, no matter how many times I successfully contorted myself into a pretzel, I was denied. Even though I had continually sacrificed my needs, wants, and desires to please them, I had failed. All my efforts. The time I wasted biting my tongue; the time I wasted giving myself pep talks before I interacted with them; the time I spent getting ready to be the most perfect version of myself; the time I spent apologizing and taking accountability for their harsh words and actions. All of it wasted.

I found myself trapped in the maze, again. It's a beautiful, elaborate, green, lush hedge maze similar to one you'd find in *Alice in Wonderland*. Throughout the time being estranged from my closest family members, I've momentarily escaped the maze, or at least, thought I'd found my way out, only to discover – with an interaction with a family member – I was thrust back inside.

I'd search endlessly for a way out of the pain I was experiencing due to the interaction, or due to a memory resurfacing that I'd pushed too far inside for too many years. I'd have to walk through the maze, searching for an escape from the emotional pain spurred by the encounter or the memory.

I'd find all sorts of dead ends only to end up right where I'd started. I'd walk circles trying to figure out how I could fix a situation or what I could do to bring peace in God's terms. Should I write a letter? Should I send a heartfelt text or gift? "God, what can I do to fix this?" I'd cry out into my pillow, before drifting to sleep.

I found comfort in the story of the unjust judge from Luke Chapter 18. A widow's rights were being violated and she needed protection, but the judge wouldn't give her the time of day. Even so, she never stopped badgering him and asking for his help and assistance. The judge didn't care about God or even what other people thought, but simply because she persisted in asking for help, he finally assisted her and she got what she needed. I decided that I would follow the widow's example in my relationship with God.

Isaiah 30:18-9 (NIV) tells us, "The Lord longs to be gracious to you; therefore, he will rise up to show you compassion. For the Lord is a God of justice. Blessed are all who wait for him!"

I ask Him daily to bless my mother and the rest of my family members and to bring God's justice to my relationships. I have decided to never stop warring daily with love for them. I also have chosen to forgive each family member nightly if anger or resentment creeps back into my heart.

Alone, sitting on the grassy floor of the maze, I made the choice to surrender, fully aware of my limited human capabilities in a situation so much bigger than myself: **I could not get myself out of the maze and I could not fix my family**. I came to the realization that I could walk a million circles around the maze trying to figure out what I could change to escape the standstill of a situation with my closest family members. I gave up trying all of my ways, trying to understand, and begged for rest.

I prayed, "I know the only way out is through you, Jesus. You are the way."

That's when I saw Him.

Standing there clothed in white linen and a red sash, He extended his hand and offered it to me. I'd spent hours upon hours surveying the height of the maze, its depths, re-examining the paths I'd already traveled, and thinking if I turned a different way, it would lead me out. Exhausted, defeated, and realizing that I had been working so hard only to get nowhere, I took His hand and stood up.

He led me towards the exit. The path to leave was not as complicated as I'd made it out to be, in actuality; no, it was like a simple, welcome, refreshing breeze. I wasn't laboring and perplexed any longer. I was relaxed, confident, and enjoying my stroll, even for the first time able to take in the beauty of the maze all around me.

Before I knew it, we had left the maze behind, and I found myself in new, open spaces no longer confined by the walls of the maze.

I was sitting on the couch with Vada having a princess movie marathon, and suddenly, seemingly out of nowhere, I felt discontent about staying at home. It was an odd feeling for me because leading up to that point, I'd felt completely content with not working for the past four-and-a-half years.

I heard, clear as day, "I have a job for you," and knew it was the Lord.

He told me to get on a specific search engine, and I scrolled the jobs in my location before I came across one that grabbed my attention. It was for an administrative assistant at a local plumbing company. I knew nothing about plumbing, but I felt certain this was the job He had for me and didn't hesitate to forward it to Brett.

He replied "I know these people. I went to high school with the owner's sister."

He placed a call for me on Monday, and I had an interview that Thursday for the position. Clearly, working at a plumbing company was not the most glamourous role I could have hoped for, but I was genuinely excited.

I was still in persistent pain and got fatigued very easily, but had stopped my search for medical explanations. In fact, I had stopped all medications except one for migraines, and was better able to function than previously, but was still deeply grieving over the loss of communication with family. This position was forty hours a week, Monday through Friday, and I doubted I could do it. But I trusted that if He had it for me, He would give me the energy.

Two slow weeks passed with me looking at my phone constantly for confirmation and finally, it rang! I was offered the position and started the following Monday. We didn't particularly need the money at the time, as restaurant owners, so I was confused why I was working in the first place, but trusted God anyway and showed up daily. I knew I had to be at this job for a reason.

While working one day at my desk, I received a text from my mother that my grandfather had died. I couldn't believe she'd conveyed the sensitive information via a text, but also, I couldn't believe he was gone, so it was a twofold, deep pain that overwhelmed me in that moment. I was in shock.

The day of my grandfather's celebration of life was fast approaching, and on the eve of his celebration, my phone rang. I saw "MOM" to identify the caller and felt panicked, but hopeful. Maybe this was the conversation we'd been needing to have, and maybe all would be well. Looking at Brett, I timidly answered.

"Hello..."

I was cut off. "How could you take the presents I got for you and not come to Thanksgiving at my house, and how dare you, and are you even going to show up at your grandfather's funeral and..."

She was yelling so loudly I had to hold the phone away from my ear. I calmly interrupted her and said, "Mom, I love you. We will see you tomorrow. Good-bye."

I knew I had to set a hard boundary – I wasn't going to take the mistreatment from her anymore. And I was done apologizing simply to smooth everything over because she was incapable of owning her own actions, as I had done many times in the past.

Still, it was heartbreaking to feel that most of my extended family was looking down at me because of my own mother's words and weren't interested in speaking to me.

I was shaking when I walked into my grandfather's celebration of life ceremony. We walked into the room where the celebration was being held. I saw my mother for the first time, and I said hello and awkwardly hugged her. There were other people around, but by her expression I knew inside she was seething.

After we stood in a reception line to greet other attendees, we all sat down at unreserved tables. Brett and I wound up at a table all by ourselves. I was on the brink of a full-on breakdown. The reality of the situation and my grandfather's death was hitting me simultaneously, and I felt myself about to start ugly crying.

Suddenly, my cousin got up from his full table of family members and came and sat by me. His simple gesture made all the difference for me that day. He reinforced to me what I was feeling already: **One person and one singular act of kindness have the ability to change everything for someone else.**

I was deeply touched by his actions.

The announcement was made that they were going to pass a microphone around, and whoever would like to share a story about my grandpa was welcome. The words had no sooner been spoken when my mother quickly and somewhat aggressively snatched the microphone first.

She spoke bitterly of a father who did not speak much to her. Her harsh words, riddled with overtones of unforgiveness, landed on everyone in the room with heaviness. In response, a loud sigh resonated, along with some groans – human responses to the level of pain my mother was still in, and now spewing openly, at her own father's funeral.

I wondered how many understood what she was declaring in that moment. She was so ready to reveal his shortcomings as a father, she spoke first and wanted everyone in that room to know how he'd wronged her. Why is that?

And did anyone else in my family start to piece anything together at that point about the condition of her heart? To me, it was evident she wasn't sad he was dead; instead, she was mad he died on her. On top of how he mistreated her in the world, he traumatized her further with his death, leaving her to find him. She still blamed him for so many things, and I winced along with others as I now understood a bigger piece of the puzzle.

CHAPTER 25

Three Pages A Day

I continued to pray and write my three pages a day. I felt led to bring the writing forward into a book and prayed for confirmation. Exhausted from my rigorous, new, full-time gig, I went to bed abnormally early one evening. I felt a gentle rustling in my sleep and was awakened to see a vision of myself sitting at our kitchen table.

Nevada was playing by my feet, and she did not look much older than she was currently. I was reading a book in my hand, and I was shown a fresh page ripped directly from the book with typed writing.

I couldn't make out the specific words, but it was imparted to me while watching the vision that this was my completed book, finished and published. God was showing me another lived moment from my own future that I hadn't experienced yet in my time. He was using my memories from the future to encourage and confirm the things He was speaking to me in the present.

I now had the miraculous confirmation that I was going to become a published author, and the handwritten pages in my notebooks would be made available for public consumption. But I had no idea how that was going to happen.

I didn't know a publisher or how to go about getting a book published. At this point, I didn't even know what my book was going to be about, or even my own story. Each day I sat down with a pen and my notebook, I did not know what the next three pages would be filled with; I just trusted that God would work through me and enable me to write what He intended for that particular day.

I would be continually surprised by the words that flowed from my pen and sometimes I kept writing past my original three pages. I started to understand that the "how" wasn't as important as the commitment I had made – and when I said 'yes' and honored the process, God ensured the "how" fell into place for that particular day.

I started to understand that God would connect me with the right people to bring my book forward, and I focused on what I could control, which was the writing portion.

I noticed that as I remained consistent to write three pages no matter what my day brought, a new fierceness was being forged inside me. He had instilled a burning, passionate desire to continue on a path that I did not know, though I knew I was supposed to be on it, come what may. I now possessed a faith and foundation cemented in the fires of pain, adversity, and abuse, and I would not stop until I saw where this was going to go, regardless of what others thought, or what they said, or if they believed in me or not.

I decided that I believed God. I am a writer. It was always He who nurtured me when the day had brought such unbearable circumstances to light. He held me and I released the traumatic events of my past, one story at a time, one day at a time.

Some days, my writing brought insurmountable joy as I wrote about victories I had experienced, or fond memories with my children and husband. I'd have an extra pep in my step as my writing revealed that I had a lot of blessings in my life to count. I'd rejoice when I discovered a new insight into myself, feeling like I had uncovered another piece to my own story.

My kids would get sick, or a day would not go according to plan, as life so frequently has a tendency to do, but I found there was always a time slot for my writing, if I was persistent and creative. Somedays I'd have time to only write a page before I'd get interrupted, but I'd pick it back up when I could grab another free moment.

My tenacity in this regard started to invade my life as my writing continued. I started working out on a more regular basis and started to see other areas in my life where I could improve with more dedication to a consistent approach. My husband and I started to make a more concerted effort towards communicating, and our marriage has also greatly improved as a result.

I was able to gain perspective on my own journey by reflecting and reading through my own experiences. Some days, I wrote when I was processing hurt toward a family member – and upon rereading this, I saw the opportunity to forgive and work through the pain I'd missed the first time, lost in my own hurt. Through openly venting on the pages, I could go back and see my growth in certain areas and target others where I remained stagnant.

As I wrote specifically about multiple scenarios and my writing culminated, a bigger-picture story started to come into focus on the pages. I was beginning to understand that my healing wasn't dependent on other family members coming back into my life. I was making progress, finding my stride, and starting to step into my purpose as a writer. Where I had once felt uncertain, I was gaining confidence and starting to stand on God's promises and my new identity in Him.

As my story emerged on the pages, I also stopped seeing my mother as a victim. My perspective shifted, and instead, I saw I had let my mother define me and was motivated and driven by fear in many aspects of my life that I would displease her.

By writing my story, I was keeping a record of my lived life that spoke specifically to my thoughts, my dreams, and my life experiences. My children and the generations to follow will forever have a glimpse into my heart and know more about where they came from: a gift I would have given anything to have, especially from my biological father.

As I continued to honor my agreement to write three pages and time progressed, I started to feel healing in places where I had been wounded. I could read my own writing and moments about growing up and not feel such intense pain. This astounded me. When I wrote the content originally, I was torn up inside and tears poured onto the pages, smearing my ink on many occasions. But God was healing me as I confronted my past and present situations via processing them on the pages.

On days where I was struggling or needing additional encouragement, my own written words days or months earlier comforted me. I drew fresh strength from my writing capabilities to continue on my journey. Soon, I wasn't needing to use as many words to describe scenarios and noticed my writing was getting crisper and more concise. Words that I did not know would often pop into my head as I wrote. I would look them up online and discover the definition to be perfect for the context I was currently writing. This continues to happen continually, and I know it is God helping me to accomplish the task that He has assigned: this book.

Meanwhile, it was becoming painstakingly evident that my job was not going to be a fit for me long term. Everything about this office was out of date: the décor, the technology, and the culture. As the only female employee, I was being mistreated. The more I prayed following my departure in late February of 2020, the more I heard, "I have checks in the mail coming for you."

I was so confused. Who was going to send these checks?

I went out to our mailbox day after day looking for the mysterious payments, but didn't understand what I was hearing until the beginning of March, when I heard, "file for unemployment."

Then the pandemic hit. We own a restaurant, and people were no longer going to be sitting inside eating, financially affecting us. But suddenly, my unemployment had been approved, and we had checks coming in the mail.

They said they were tacking on an extra $600 per check, making it more than I'd made while I was working at the plumbing company. Brett and I were awestruck that God had prompted me to even apply for unemployment before the pandemic rush.

God knew the pandemic was coming, and thanks to that job, we now had the extra income. My unemployment was providing a buffer from lost revenue due to the restaurant being mandated to stop indoor dining.

I had been so upset working there, and I didn't understand the point, but I did know that I was hearing Him and He confirmed everything with those checks in the mail. I was beginning to understand that not everything God had for me was going to give me the warm fuzzies, but that there was always going to be reason and purpose in His assignments, even if I didn't know it at the time.

CHAPTER 26

Rewind and Reflect

One Sunday in late August 2020, I decided to watch a documentary called *Rewind*. The premise is "digging through his father's home videos, a young man reconstructs his story of his boyhood and recalls the abuse he suffered through."

As I watched him recounting the details of his own abuse, it was as if a flash drive was downloaded into my brain. All of my memories regarding my own sexual abuse were suddenly unlocked. They flashed before my eyes and I remembered what I knew I had buried and forgotten.

I remembered "the childhood game" a neighbor girl introduced me to. I remembered my mom and that day at the gynecologist. I remembered everything.

I walked around for years feeling like there was something going on that I couldn't figure out. Like there was a thought, but it was just out of my reach. I felt deeply frustrated with something that felt buried, just below the surface, and I didn't have access to it.

Now the haze cleared, the fog lifted, and I knew what I had forgotten, finally.

My thoughts turned to my dad, Paul. I immediately knew I was going to write about my repressed memories surfacing and called to speak to him. I was saddened to learn that it was also the very same day my stepmother had filed for divorce from him.

I never thought that the one-sided conversation with my mother when she told me who sexually abused me had traveled further than the confines of the vehicle. I never considered the idea that anyone else knew because it hadn't been mentioned again to me all these years. Horrified, I listened as my father recounted the gritty details of being confronted by his newly married wife with the terrible accusation. My father rightfully denied it, but in my opinion, the damage to their marriage had already been done.

I cried as my father said, "Kenzie, I never blamed you and I knew it wasn't you who had done this."

My father had stood, silent and defenseless, against the terrifying accusation that he'd molested his daughter for twenty years.

I felt sick and enraged as it hit me that so many had been discussing my sexual abuse, while me, the one who had endured it, was not even aware of it herself.

I am grateful God blessed me with ability to put my feelings and emotions into words so I could continue to process and work though forgiving various family members. I discovered I did not need their apology or acknowledgement to heal, and that continues to be a powerful key as I walk out estrangement.

Writing this book has and continues to help me heal as I work through the manuscript, and I am hopeful it will lend you some powerful insight that just may be the key you've been looking for to unlock flying to new heights of self-discovery.

My story started to make a lot more sense once the tiny submarines carrying my buried trauma and experiences started to emerge from the depths and reveal their contents. I started to recall more and more of them as the time progressed and I kept writing. I was able to more fully understand the fuzzy, staticky, jumbled feeling I had when my brother or sister would refer to a memory from childhood.

I thought I simply had a bad memory but accompanying my inability to recall was something more; like a sinking, disparaging feeling layered underneath. Now that I am able to freely process my memories, I have experienced unparalleled healing from childhood traumas that I endured.

My physical pain has lifted as I have confronted the suppressed memories, and I've been able to stop going to all the doctor appointments. Sure, some of the physical pain I was experiencing, like my jaw and back, was real, solidified, physical pain. But the heaviness, the extreme exhaustion and fatigue that plagued me, I now attribute as a manifestation of all of the emotional, unprocessed pain I was experiencing while feeling suppressed. My energy levels are being restored as I heal because I am now surrounding myself with family and friends who are supportive. I am able to speak openly and share my story without breaking down because I can see the beauty in my journey and in all of the pain when I can encourage others.

I find joy and healing when I look into the eyes of my own children. Knowing my full story and coming to terms with how I was raised has helped me become a better mother. They are free from the restraints of being told they are bad or not good enough, and I remind them constantly that, "I love you all the time." I want them to know that regardless of their behavior or actions, my love offered to them is unconditional and not dependent on anything else but the fact that they are my children. Period, end of story.

I may not like their behavior or their choices on a particular day, but my love is not contingent or attached to circumstances or emotions. I will never leave or abandon them because they disagree with me. I understand that my children are not exact replicas of me and have their own strengths that need to be nurtured, and I enjoy learning about who they are becoming every day. My children have taught me a great deal about life and have made me a better person in the process because I make an effort to hear them speak and am humble enough to understand parenting isn't a one-way street.

I also ask a lot of questions – maybe too many, if you're asking my kids on a given day!

I am so grateful for the Lord and am moved by His goodness to thank Him for releasing me from the shadows of confusion, for revealing and lifting the haze surrounding me, and for clarifying and shining the light in the dark places that had been shoved deep down and forgotten.

I know firsthand the ability someone's story has to impact another life. I prayed and thought long and hard about divulging the details in this book and felt that any judgment coming my way would be outweighed by the potential to help another person feel heard or to recognize that their own physical pain could possibly be coming from emotional trauma.

Putting my intimate life details out publicly is worth it if one person who reads this feels his or her life is valuable, that he or she matters, and is loved beyond comprehension.

Maybe, if you're like me, this book might be triggering some repressed memories, and if so, I'm writing my story so you know that there is hope and healing on the other side.

Rewinding through my own story, I wish I would have paid more attention to how I was feeling after my interactions with others. I often ignored and pushed down feelings of inadequacy after interactions with people who made me feel I simply didn't measure up or couldn't do anything right. If you are feeling depleted, put down, upset, or depressed after an interaction, make sure you pay attention to your feelings without automatically dismissing them.

I believe after years and years of exposure to family members and some friendships, my body was telling me what my mind didn't want to believe in the form of expressing it physically. I think I thought I could "handle" my mother or a difficult friend, but the truth was, their demeaning attitude towards me combined with my silence as a response was taking a toll on my health.

If you are feeling especially run down, rewind your day and take stock of your emotional state. Who did you interact with? What did you discuss? How did you feel? I am very cognizant of my state after speaking with a friend or family member now because I intentionally ask questions about my emotional state and listen to my body. It's never too late to start over or to stand up for yourself and take some time to reflect and rewind.

CHAPTER 27

New Life

One day, The Lord spoke to me as I sat crumpled on the floor, desperate to be heard and seen by my family. I saw myself and my family members suspended in space, weightless, against a backdrop of night sky and so many stars. The expressions on their faces were frozen and complacent as they floated.

I, however, was desperately trying to hang onto them with my left hand; panicked and grabbing at them in an effort to keep them with me. They were not returning my efforts, and I knew it, but hung onto them with all my might, offering to do all the work, even when they would not. Pleading in vain.

Then, to my right, He appeared.

"Let them go," Jesus softly beckoned, holding out His hand.

I cried harder, realizing I'd been hopelessly holding onto them this whole time.

"Leave them behind and come with me," He said. "There's work to be done."

Realizing I could no longer take them with me, I watched their faces as I let go of their hands with my left hand and took Jesus's with my right. As He led me onward, I watched them slip away while they remained peacefully suspended in thin air as if unaware that I had let go.

"Time is short, and there is much work to be done in my kingdom," Jesus spoke.

I got the impression that things with my family are not over. No, they are to be continued. Through the painful process of refinement, He has introduced me to the person He created, step by step, and I am feeling this strength and peace that I had never known before He came flooding into my life.

I have to admit that I feel like I can breathe clean air for the first time. The flames and the fires are behind me, I'm no longer choking on the smoke, and God has breathed new life into it all. I have found myself in unfamiliar, new territory without the angst of wondering when my mother will start another fire. I am no longer expected to suit up and tackle the flames, since I've decided I'm not putting out any more fires. I have found reprieve from the exhaustion of tiptoeing around and doing my best to get everything right in accordance with her ever-changing standards for my life.

The truth was, that suit was never really protecting me; it was a façade and an illusion to think I could fix anything on my own. In reality, I had suffered so many severe burns in that suit that it was in tatters and practically unusable. I was a lousy firefighter on my own. When I finally realized He'd been with me all along, waiting for me to surrender my firefighter suit, I took it off, surrendering completely to Him, meeting Him in the flames. I stepped into the fire, met His gaze, and rested in His arms. To my great surprise, I was not burned. Instead, I became one with the flames, and He used the fire to refine, purify, and heal me.

The same flames that should have destroyed me made me who I am today: completely redeemed in Jesus, a phoenix rising from the ashes. A new creation.

Malachi 3:2 (TMT) says, "But who will be able to stand up to that coming? Who can survive his appearance? He'll be like white-hot fire from the smelter's furnace. He'll be like the strongest lye soap at the laundry. He'll take his place as a refiner of silver, as a cleanser of dirty clothes."

I stayed committed to what God had called me to do, regardless of the opinions of family members, and trusted that God was going to align me with supportive, encouraging people to help me along in this new adventure – even though I did not know who they would be or when they would be brought into my life.

As I continued to write, I prayed about how my book was going to be published and connected with Rebecca Hall Gruyter, the CEO of RHG Media Productions. Instantly, I felt a connection to her personally. Through our phone calls, I could feel God working behind the scenes. I felt she was a friend I had known for a lot longer. I knew I could trust her with my story, and she was uniquely gifted with the exact skillset and ability to craft a process to bring my book to the masses.

As we continued to work together on this book, I got another opportunity to work with her and other coauthors on the anthology, *Step into Your Brilliant Purpose*. I discovered a community of like-minded individuals from a variety of backgrounds looking to help others through their shared experiences as well.

As a result of our combined efforts, I became a number one best-selling international author. My chapter, "Let Forgiveness Color Your World," speaks in detail about how I missed out on getting to know my dad, Paul, the one who adopted me the day I was born because I was too distracted and scared by my mother's narrative about my biological father to have a close relationship with him. We'd been deprived the ability to truly connect, until now.

Over the course of the past few years, we've communicated about my upbringing and have had very insightful, loving, productive conversations that have brought us closer than we have ever been. My dad has fully and wholeheartedly supported me throughout my writing process. He's always happy for me when I have a speaking or writing engagement, and he listens and gives excellent feedback. I continue to be blown away by my dad's ability to forgive others, no matter how deeply they have wounded him. He truly tries to walk his life out from a perspective of healing and gratitude, and our renewed relationship gives me a lot of strength and hope for healing in relationships with other family members where we are still estranged.

I am extremely proud of the man my father is today and thankful that God made a way where I could be his daughter.

Around the same time I started working with Rebecca, I got connected to my personal trainer, Yvonne Greer. She wasn't simply interested in my physical well-being – she understands the body, mind, and soul connection and has worked hard to help me feel supported in my entire being as a person.

Thanks to workouts with her, my back pain has decreased significantly, to the point where it is no longer an issue currently. She has shown me what a huge impact one person can make in a life and has emboldened me to continue writing, hoping that I can inspire and help someone the way she and the community at PowerZone have helped me.

Rebecca and I enjoyed working together on these projects so much she graciously offered me a position with RHG Media, where I am currently now employed. It is another reminder for me that we never fully know what will happen or what opportunities will arise when we are open to sharing our lives and hearts with others.

I would have missed out on so much had I let the fear of what others thought hold me back from speaking out and sharing my story. Now, I get to look forward to more doors that I know God will open along this exciting new journey I am on as a writer, and hopefully how sharing my story has impacted others. And I continue to pray I will have the opportunity to start Chloe's House one day.

I'm in the process of launching a program to help others write their three pages a day, to be able to process their story and life, and possibly bring their story forward too. I continue to write and see what is being birthed and being called forward. I'm open to speaking and sharing when those opportunities come that I can share and make a difference.

If writing three pages calls to you and you would like support in writing your pages, please reach out to me and I would be honored to support you on your journey. In addition, consider purchasing the journal that accompanies my story specifically formatted to help you write three pages a day.

I will always have hope in my heart for reconciliation and restoration with family members I am not currently in communication with. I continue to make the effort to reach out, as I feel prompted to have conversations to put us on the path to healing. A successful relationship requires a concerted effort and an openness to partake in meaningful, respectful conversations from both people involved, and unfortunately my advances have gone unrequited to date. Regardless, the silver lining in my extended family for now continues to be the close relationship I now share with Paul.

I find strength in focusing on those who are supporting and participating in my life and focus on the relationships with those who are willing to walk out life side-by-side with me.

My faith continues to flourish, despite not currently being connected to a church. I'm open to the prospect of reconnecting with a church in the future and will never entirely rule anything out because I know with God, all things are possible. I continue to experience miracle after miracle in my life, through visions, through dreams, and through things happening that I couldn't explain other than to sit and reflect with awe on the Lord and what He is doing. I find so much joy in knowing that every promise He makes is true, and that He always keeps His word. I know He has so many more people for me like Rebecca and Yvonne, who truly live every day to help others and make a difference in others' lives, and I hope to pay that forward through this book and through the other avenues where I am called.

I believe each one of us is special, unique, and worthy, and that you possess a capability that no one else can: to see the world through your own eyes. Perspective is everything. The very same areas where you have been held back and hurt can be utilized to build your wings and help you soar.

My health continues to improve as I write, speak out, process, and heal from years of repressed trauma, and surround myself with people who are intentional about lifting others up and helping each other along in our journeys.

There are so many more words and experiences I left on the cutting room floor of my journey when writing this book. I hope you know you aren't alone, no matter what you're walking through and no matter how much pain you may be in; there is healing on the other side.

If you'd like to connect, reach out, and I'd love to speak with you about how I can help you on your own journey. May you grow your wings and soar! God bless.

CLOSING THOUGHTS

Thank you so much for taking the time to read my book. I hope it has encouraged you to see your circumstances from a different point of view, to feel empowered to pursue your destiny, and to better understand your own journey.

I hope you have taken the time to explore my "Pinion Points to Help You Grow Your Wings" to help you fly higher as you continue to adventure through your life. If you have reflected on the Pinion Points and would like more of an opportunity to heal, or to gain further personal insight from this book, please consider purchasing my companion journal, where you will be able to learn more about how writing three pages a day can change your life, as it has mine.

Whether you are simply looking to record an account of your life, heal, improve your writing capabilities, and/or maybe to write your own story, you will be blown by how drastically everything can change when you say YES and commit to taking action in this one small area.

I hope my story has inspired you to realize that you may not have the ability to change your circumstances, but you have the ability to use the things that you may view negatively and change your perspective. You can change your view to your advantage to flip the script of your life if you are willing to change your perspective. The same places that were once used to bring you down can be used to help you to build your wings and soar if you are open to leaning in and seeing things from a different point of view.

We all go through painful experiences, but we can use them and find meaning and purpose by allowing them to refine and sharpen our lives if we are willing to allow God to work through them and eliminate the excess. Hope and healing are not only possible, they are guaranteed when you war by staying persistent and refuse to accept nothing less.

I believe I am only getting started, and I'm looking forward to writing, speaking, and sharing more in-depth about my journey and story in the future, so I hope you will stay connected with me moving forward.

What was the biggest takeaway for you from my story? I would love to hear from you about the information you found that was most helpful to you as you read my story and insights. If you have follow-up questions, would like to be personally coached about how you can start your own journey writing three pages a day, or are just needing some additional encouragement along your own journey, I am also available to connect with for a free thirty-minute session if you would like a personalized, confidential conversation with me via my website: www.https://mackenziekaynelson.com.

I also have more plans available if you feel our connection is helpful and would like coaching in a certain aspect of your life on a more consistent basis.

Another great resource to purchase if you're looking for further information on how to overcome fear and step out and shine is the number one international best-selling anthology, *Step into Your Brilliant Purpose*, compiled by Rebecca Hall Gruyter and Maureen Ryan Blake. I am one of seventeen experts featured, with my chapter, "Let Forgiveness Color Your World," bringing further depth and detail to my story while offering insight for your own journey. There's also a *Step into Your Brilliant Purpose* companion journal for purchase where you can write down your thoughts as you read through the powerful stories to get the most out of the book. May you grow your wings and soar!

With Heartfelt Thanks,
MacKenzie

ACKNOWLEDGMENTS

First, I'd like to say thank you to God. He is the entire reason this book has been published in the first place and all glory goes to Him for making this possible.

Thank you so much to my wonderful husband, Brett. I could not have worked the endless hours this manuscript has required without your support, encouragement, and endless hours spent keeping our children entertained while "Mom is writing, *again*?!"

Thank you to my son, Lincoln, eleven, and my daughter Nevada, five, for teaching me so much about faith, hope, love, and God. I continue to learn more lessons daily through your innocent perspectives and huge hearts for helping others. Thank you for sacrificing your time with Mom so I could heal and help others along my journey.

Thank you to the amazing team and community at RHG Media Productions, and to Rebecca Hall Gruyter specifically for your friendship, guidance, and help bringing my story to life.

Huge thank-you's to my dad, Paul, and both my mother- and father-in-law (Bob and Jan) for your acceptance and support along this process, as well as my sister and brother-in-law for your kindness.

Jennifer, Mary, Chelsea, Yvonne, Raechelle, Cassie, Dylan, Gretchen, Jackie, and Barb: The conversations we've shared and your friendships along this journey have touched my life and given me strength and encouragement to keep going in this process.

I'd also like to thank you, the reader, for purchasing my book and investing your time to learn about my story and insights. I hope you learn more about yourself through my story and feel emboldened to spread your wings and fly!

With Love,
MacKenzie

PINION POINTS TO HELP YOU GROW YOUR WINGS

According to Collinsdictonary.com, when described as a noun, a pinion is simply the part of a bird's wing, including the flight feathers. Interestingly enough, when used as a verb, the definition changes and takes on new meaning: to make a bird incapable of flight by removing that part (of the wing) from which the flight feathers grow.

The areas in my life that once clipped my wings and prevented me from flying have now transitioned to take on new meaning and become the ones where I've found freedom and am now able to soar, thanks to shifting my perspective to fly higher.

I hope these insights I have discovered along my journey enable you to see your circumstances from a different point of view, so that you, too, can discover renewed strength in the same areas where you were once held down. It's time to soar!

Chapter 1: Introduction: Born of Fire

As a child, I had very little control over my life. What my mother said went, and I was forced against my own will to submit to her whims and desires. Now as an adult, I have learned that there was something I possessed all along that no one could take: my own perspective. The lens I view the world through is mine, along with my story. No one can experience your journey through your lenses. If someone has stolen your voice, it's not too late to speak up and tell your own story with your own words and through your own unique perspective.

Chapter 2: Family Dynamics

The definition of "unfathomable" is impossible to comprehend. I believe in the span of a human life you are quite the exception if you do not run into one such event within the scope of your own existence on the Earth. Trials are sure to come, and when they do, how we choose to view them can be the key to ushering in healing. We do not have control over so many facets of life, but choosing to grow despite unfathomable challenges, events, and circumstances is within your grasp. If you are in the midst of a crisis in your own life, there is hope.

Chapter 3: Church, Family, and Basketball

Looks can be deceiving. Sometimes a polished veneer only serves to cover up the corruption that rots just beneath the surface. I was trained as a child to listen to words and ignore actions. Words were the polished veneer that constantly covered up and excused the abusive actions. When someone was not true to their words, I assumed I was to blame for their failure. In your relationships with others, do you trust in words alone? You are not at fault if someone is not delivering on their promises with actions.

Chapter 4: Born to Stand Out

I found my superpower … and it's the same as yours. You were not born to follow a crowd and simply go along with what everyone else thinks, no. You were made for more and so was I. We share the same superpower: No one can be you and no one can be me. We each carry something special inside that only we can use to impact and change the world for the better. One way I recently discovered how to express my superpower is by writing. Have you thought about the hidden talents you may possess that have the ability to change the world? If not, what's stopping you from exploring?

Chapter 5: God, *The Matrix*, and Destiny

Distraction used to be a close friend of mine, for many years. Distraction liked to keep me occupied and looking the other way when true pain and conflict rose to the forefront, and I felt too uncomfortable to face my circumstances. Distraction seemed fun, until I realized in recent years that our friendship was keeping me too busy to meet my new best friends Healing and Hope. I had to cut ties with Distraction to forge new connections to step into my brilliant purpose. Are there areas in your life where you're letting Distraction keep you too occupied to meet your new best friend, Destiny?

Chapter 6: Cuddles

When the unexpected occurs, life as we know it can get turned upside down and send us reeling. We are forced into a space where we try to survive based on the knowledge of the world we have acquired. Our decision as to how to proceed next varies from person to person depending on the perspective the individual possesses in relation to their circumstances. Perspectives can be changed, and therefore, so can the outcomes in your future. What perspective are you choosing?

Chapter 7: My Choice

Is there a burden you carry that's been deemed too difficult to talk about? Do you currently suffer in silence? If so, that pain will never recede until you can find your voice and an outlet to share your emotions. You are worthy, you matter, and you deserve to be heard.

Chapter 8: Healing, Love, and School

What are your beliefs in God? Not what you've heard in church or school, not what someone else told you to think, but your own thoughts? Do you have a personal faith? If you have questions about God, do you ask Him directly, or do you rely on people for answers?

Chapter 9: Lincoln and My Grandfather

    The thing about life is that nothing stays the same. Dependent on the scenario you apply those words to, they can elicit feelings of sadness or joy. Life can be so spectacular that we wish the moment in time would freeze and allow us to sustain the feeling of ecstasy forever, but still, it passes. The same is said of the very hardest moments in life. It is a gift of mercy that they too shall pass. Unexpectedly, I have found that it is in my hardest moments where I have drawn the most strength for my future.

Chapter 10: My Brother's Wedding

    I used to focus on the people who weren't supporting me more than the ones who showed up for me, which left me feeling alone and unsatisfied. Now, I am intentional about focusing and celebrating the supportive people actively contributing positively to my life. Who are you focused on? The ones who are absent or the ones who are present? Perspective matters.

Chapter 11: Sins of the Father

    We can arrive at the same destination as someone else even though we may take a different road and a few detours and get lost completely along the way. I believe there is purpose in all of it if we are willing to search. Each of us are on our own amazing journey that is exclusively ours to own. Are you fully embracing the journey...not just focused on the destination?

Chapter 12: Medical Challenges and Nevada

    If I've learned one thing in life, in the past, oftentimes my expectation of a situation did not match the reality. I used to invest heavily in happy endings in my own life; something I drew from the fantasy of Disney princess movies growing up. It was painful at first, to let go of my idea of happiness in accordance with what the world and movies taught me to expect, but now I find it freeing. Are there any areas of your life where you're still holding on to unrealistic expectations and feeling disappointed? How can you shift to be in more alignment with your expectations?

Chapter 13: Tell Mom, "She is Going to be Okay."

Is there someone you're hesitant to forgive because you feel like you're letting them off the hook and they don't deserve it? Shift your perspective: Forgiveness isn't for that person. It's for you to unleash healing in your own life. If you're curious, try the exercise that jumpstarted my journey. Find a quiet space. Take a few deep breaths in and out, and when you're ready, picture the jail cell. Ask God if there is anyone you need to forgive and watch to see who populates the cell. If someone does, release them, forgive them, and free yourself in the process.

Chapter 14: Chronic Pain

My chronic pain condition alerted me to the fact that so many were only listening for their opportunity to add to the conversation instead of truly investing and being present in the conversation with me. I have no control over others, but I did take this realization and turn it inward to reflect on myself and my behavior as I engage in conversations with others. Am I listening because I'm waiting for my opportunity to be heard, or am I listening to learn something about someone else and help them to feel truly heard, valued, and supported? Are you truly listening and being present in your conversations?

Chapter 15: Italy

I let fear and threats hold me back from pursuing the whereabouts of my biological father for the majority of my life, something I think I will always regret. Simultaneously, facing this fear set me free from the constant state of wondering that had held me captive and taught me an important lesson in the process: If fear is at the root of a reason why you are not pursuing something you have a desire and a drive to accomplish, do it anyway. Freedom is on the other side of fear, not more fear.

Chapter 16: Pain and Freedom

When someone in your life encounters a strange situation that you have not personally experienced, how do you react? With cynicism because their experience has been different than yours, or with curiosity, from a place of wanting to learn more about the brave person stepping out and risking "sounding weird" by sharing with you? Life can be awkward, bizarre, and sometimes difficult to make sense of, but we are all in this together. How can you hold a space and understanding for others as well as for yourself?

Chapter 17: One Day at a Time

At some point in our lives, we are likely to be confronted with our mortality via some form of a health issue. When these issues arise in the lives of your friends and loved ones, how do you show your support? I desperately wanted someone to simply sit with me. That's all. I didn't want gifts or advice, but longed for simple, quiet acceptance in the midst of all of the questioning and uncertainty. How can you support others and truly be with them?

Chapter 18: Gold Crosses

I recognize that we are each at different places in our faith journey, and regardless of where you are as you read, I hope you know how loved you are in the very place where you sit today. There's nothing more you have to do. Let that wash over you for a moment. Love without condition, regardless of what you do or do not believe. Love regardless of what you have done or are doing. You are spectacular. You are known. You are seen. You are loved!

Chapter 19: The Encounter

I have heard stories from others about experiencing a spiritual awakening that happened overnight, which have encouraged me to share mine. I was completely transformed and awakened to a new realm I hadn't experienced and didn't know I could even access. I continue to explore and seek answers to this day about everything I experienced during that life-altering, mesmerizing encounter with Jesus. Have you experienced any kind of overnight spiritual shift in your life? If so, you're not alone and you're not weird. If you have held back from sharing your own experience with others, you're reading this now for a reason. I challenge you to start leaning in and thinking about sharing your own story.

Chapter 20: True Peace

Sometimes we feel called to take a stand and share something so private, so intimate, and so different from what others surrounding us view as normal. It could be that it has never been done before: that you are a pioneer on the front lines blazing a new path to help others. Sometimes what we feel led to do is something completely new, and that makes others uncomfortable. Is there anything you are holding back from moving forward with in your own life because others don't approve? Be willing to share what you are uniquely called to be and to share out into the world.

Chapter 21: Releasing the Excess

In the hustle and bustle of our busy culture, sometimes we can get lost in simply going through the motions. Our destiny can be held hostage by the doldrum of our routine and daily agenda. It takes a commitment to being intentional about honoring the moment you are living in now to break through the cycle and make room for originality and joy to shine in your world. Start now. Take a deep breath in, and as you breath out, picture normal, everyday actions that could use some fresh invigoration. Before your next breath, picture your most joyful memory and remember how you felt as you breathe in. Release the joy of that memory as you breathe out. Take a few more breaths if you feel led to do so and think about what destiny means to you.

Chapter 22: Chloe's House

My destiny and purpose have been found in a place I least expected to find it: an area where I have experienced my greatest pain and loss. Writing has helped me to process and heal from my old wounds, and as I surrendered them to God, He continued to help me as I released the old trauma of the past. If you are aware of an area in your life where you have experienced deep pain and have not faced it, it could be holding you back from your destiny. Your purpose might be found in your pain too.

Chapter 23: The Other Side

Perseverance has been a huge key to unlocking my writing potential. I was consistent writing three pages a day as I compiled this book, but each day brought something new. I had days where I sat and wrote and watched the letters blur together as my tears poured onto the pages. There were also days where I felt exhilarated and jubilant, only to be followed by another day where I was crushed and devastated as I wrote. I learned that to persevere, I had to stay consistent, despite my fluctuating feelings and emotions. Do you struggle with staying consistent when working toward a goal? Do you work from a place of how you feel, or do you persevere regardless?

Chapter 24: Life without Mother

Sometimes in life, we can feel like we've moved on and have a handle on a situation, only for it to reinfect our lives again. There are delicate situations such as estrangement that do not come with a handbook for neatly navigating the separation from close family members. For me, sometimes it has been a journey of one step forward, then two steps backward. However, I have learned to give myself grace and time to work towards healing in these relationships. I give myself permission to feel what I am feeling without labeling them as "right" or "wrong" feelings. Most nights, I check to make sure I have not held anything against anyone who I have felt wronged by and forgive them if I have let bitterness back into the picture. It is a daily, fluctuating journey that I have learned to embrace. How can you extend more grace to yourself and to others?

Chapter 25: Three Pages a Day

After being a stay-at-home mom exclusively for years, it certainly felt out of my comfort zone to start looking to go back to work, but I knew where I was feeling led. When I told friends and family about my new job, they seemed confused, yet I continued to pursue the path I was being led down, even if I didn't know where I was going. If I would have ignored the nudge to look for a job, I never would have gotten the rewards of the money we needed during a pandemic where our restaurant was compromised. Is there somewhere or something you've been feeling drawn to do, but it doesn't seem to make sense to you to pursue? There might be a purpose you can't see yet.

Chapter 26: Rewind and Reflect

The documentary *Rewind* showed me how important it was for me to use my voice to speak out about my pain because I was able to remember my own trauma through someone else's brave recollection of their own story. If I never remembered my own abuse, how would I be able to work through it to find healing on the other side? Finally, the haze that I suffered beneath for so long is gone, and I know what it is like to walk in clarity and truth, thanks to the bravery of the cast and crew of *Rewind*. I speak out and share my story to pay it forward in hopes that someone else can come out of the haze too. How can you use your voice to speak out, share your story, and help another?

Chapter 27: New Life

My story doesn't have the happy ending I pictured when I started writing this book, but I have learned to take life one day at a time. I no longer see beginnings and endings with the same perspective. I see everything as "to be continued," and this story is certainly no exception. We get to enjoy the journey with its ups and downs, richly embracing it all. How can you start to take one day at a time and release worrying about trying to create a "happy ending?" Today is a day to embrace and live fully.

ABOUT THE AUTHOR

MacKenzie Nelson is a #1 international best-selling author. She is a restaurant owner, book launch specialist at RHG Media Corporation, former high school all-state basketball player, and lives to bring others healing and hope through sharing her story. She resides in Peoria, IL, with her husband, Brett, her son, Lincoln, and her daughter, Vada.

For further updates and to get in touch with MacKenzie Nelson, visit:

https://www.mackenziekaynelson.com

https://www.myfathersfeathers.com

Please check out my podcast "High Voltage," available on YouTube.

https://tinyurl.com/MacKenzieNelsonYT

REVIEWS

"Like a glorious phoenix rising, My Father's Feathers details MacKenzie Nelson's courageous journey of transmuting her childhood trauma into triumph. MacKenzie brings the reader vulnerably into her process of discovering her authentic voice and of owning her power, as she embarks on a healing journey of her mind, body, and heart. This story is one that confirms 'love wins' so long as you're willing to go out and fight for it."
—Julia Harriet, MiT Builder of Homes and Dreams, Best-Selling Author

"In My Father's Feathers, readers get a glimpse into MacKenzie's courageous journey through childhood trauma and the impact it had throughout her life. This exceptional book sheds light on how psychological trauma can manifest into physical pain if left untreated. MacKenzie shares her experiences and unwavering spiritual faith with such a clear, honest vulnerability that is truly inspiring. Her resilience and internal strength are highlighted throughout the book which will resonate with many and instill hope and motivation. This book is an amazing resource for anyone looking to jumpstart their own healing and spiritual journey."
—Jennifer Logan PhD, LCPC, NCC, Therapist, LifeStance Health

"MacKenzie Nelson has proven an old adage to be true: when you change the way you look at things, the things you look at change. Believing you are unwanted and unloved can cast a shadow over everything you experience. In acknowledging her faith, MacKenzie learned to love herself and light the way to a better experience. This book reminds others that they can do the same."
—Yvonne Greer, Owner, Power Zone Personal Training

"Grab a snack and beverage. Sink into your favorite chair. Once you start reading, you'll be hooked until the final word. This book is raw and beautiful. The author reveals a gutsy vulnerability while sharing a uniquely personal story that will resonate with everyone. You will find peace, healing and joy as the story unfolds."
—Jami Webster Hall, Doctor of Jurisprudence, Modern Mom, Justice Seeker, and Book Club Aficionado

"My Father's Feathers is a powerful book about one woman's courage to be vulnerable as she shares her story of violence and abuse, to healing and finding strength through GOD. MacKenzie Nelson is a gifted writer who grabs your attention from the first page. You will laugh, you will cry, and you will fall in love with My Father's Feathers."
—**Maureen Ryan Blake, Maureen Ryan Blake Media Productions and Founder of Power of the Tribe**

"Never have I been more captivated, encouraged, and seen by a book. MacKenzie's vulnerability and honesty had me hanging on every word. Her struggles with family, womanhood, and life in general, are those which I think every woman can relate to. We've all been, are in, or will be, in a place in our life where we feel unworthy. MacKenzie's writing will lead you on a journey toward forgiveness, acceptance, and most importantly, faith. My Father's Feathers is a must read. Like sitting down with a good friend, you will feel the power of connection on every page."
—**Jackie Fahey, Stylist, Daughter, Sister, Wife, Mother, Friend, and Woman**

"In this unique story of self-discovery, MacKenzie finds healing through writing, forgiveness, and her faith. As she finds her footing and takes back her voice, MacKenzie lays pavement for her true purpose; helping others. Whether it is through her writings, visions, or Chloe's House, this woman is going to make positive changes in this world! This book encourages the reader to seek out their own truths and self-knowledge so they can be ready to serve their individual true purpose even better!"
—**Raechelle, Licensed Massage Therapist**

"What an incredibly powerful book! I highly recommend this book if you're looking to heal, be inspired, and to really connect to what it is to live as love. I would recommend this to everyone!"
—**Kara Goss, Author, Speaker, Mentor**

"This book is a journey through pain, persistence and perseverance. MacKenzie Nelson shares her heartbreaking journey as a child and shocking discoveries. She had to dig deep to believe and push through even when it appeared the odds were stacked against her. Her story is one of reflection with the hopes it can inspire others to not give up."
—**Maureen Famiano President, MEFMedia Author, Best Business Minds of Tampa Bay**

"MacKenzie's book is written simply but holds a powerful, deep message. She has given us insight into a painful life, but one with strength, power, and victory. Her dependence on God and His strength gives all who read her book encouragement and hope. Her pursuit of wholeness demonstrates a life of overcoming difficulties and achieving peace and impact."
—**Elda Robinson, Best-Selling Author of A Simple Cup of -Ty**

"From the very beginning of her life, MacKenzie has had one challenge after another thrown at her and she has overcome every one of them with grace and style! Beginning as a young girl, God has shown her that there was a purpose for her. A purpose to guide others through the same type of pain and trauma she had experienced. I've also been extremely lucky to meet MacKenzie in person and speak to her one-on-one about her life story. She is a bright light and I am proud to call her a friend."
—**Mary Horst, Contracting Executive and Friend**

www.ingramcontent.com/pod-product-compliance
Lightning Source LLC
Chambersburg PA
CBHW050324010526
44119CB00003B/100